DISNEYLAND PARIS 2024

A Travel Guide to Beautiful Theme Parks and Attractions in France

By: Camille Corren

Copyright© 2023 Camille Corren
All rights reserved

Introduction:

FastPass and tickets

Amusements

Fantasyland

The Sleeping Beauty

Peter Pan's Flight

Alice in Wonderland

Discovery Land

Frontier land

Big Thunder Mountain

Adventure Land

Resorts

Chapter 1

Historical Highlights: History And Chronology Of France

Chapter 2

Plan Your Trip To Disneyland

Making Travel Plans to France

• Entry Requirements And Visas

• Consulates and Embassies

• Travel

• Safety And Health

• Budgeting And Finances

• Reading Material

Chapter 3

Best Time Of Year To Visit Disneyland Resorts

France's Weather

France's High And Low Seasons

France's Events and Festivals

Nice several dates for the funfair

Chapter 4

France's Top Restaurants

Top Cafebars France's Best Cafes And Bars

Chapter 5
Useful Phrases: French Expressions and Pronunciations to Use.

Chapter 6
The Best Hotels In France
Disneyland Hotels And Lodge

Chapter 7
101 Disneyland Paris Tips: Tips And Tricks

Chapter 8
Disneyland Parks
What Will Be Added To Disneyland Paris In 2024 And Beyond.
Near & Future Additions
Imaginative Resorts
Relatively Recent Additions

Introduction

A trip to an amusement park, such as Disneyland Paris, always leaves a positive impression and the most treasured recollections. Disneyland Paris is a non-stop celebration with a lot of attractions to amuse everyone, from young children to the elderly. It is well known for its rides, live-action movie sets, and real-life depictions of beloved Disney characters.

The Walt Disney Studio Park and Disneyland Paris are the two parks that make up Disneyland Paris. Given that Disneyland Park offers 40 attractions and The Walt Disney just has 15, which necessitates less planning, I advise Disneyland Park over The Walt Disney Park for an itinerary packed with activities.

Additionally, Disneyland Park is meticulous and has classic attractions.

A trip to an amusement park, such as Disneyland Paris, always leaves a positive impression and the most treasured recollections. Disneyland Paris is a non-stop celebration with a lot of attractions to amuse everyone, from young children to the elderly. It is well known for its rides, live-action movie sets, and real-life depictions of beloved Disney characters.

A trip to Disneyland Paris can be arranged based on a variety of variables, including events, the weather, crowds, and more. In addition to other events like Marvel Summer of Superheroes and Season of the Force: Star Wars, Disneyland Paris organizes and celebrates a wide range of occasions throughout the year, including Halloween in October, Christmas in November, and Season of the Force: Star Wars. Throughout the year, there are numerous other unplanned gatherings, food and wine festivals. When organizing your trip, you might wish to keep these in mind. Consider this while making travel plans, especially from December to February, as Paris winters may be cold and icy, which could prevent some rides at Disneyland Paris from operating. If you are, by chance, at Disneyland Paris at this time, you can always make up for the bad weather by enjoying the lovely surroundings and taking some amazing photos. Some attractions can be closed on the day of your visit due to maintenance needs. You can do this in advance by asking the authorities or going to the official Disney website. No matter how crowded it is, you could still spend two or three days exploring the park. Paris's location meant that there would frequently be a big influx of European tourists in the Park. To avoid excessive crowd levels, tourists who dislike crowds or are afraid of them should take this factor into account.

Even the journey there and back can be interesting. Flying is the ideal means of transportation for people who are visiting from outside of Europe or distant locations inside Europe. In order to get to Disneyland Paris from the CDG airport in Paris, a 10-minute train ride is all that is necessary.

Disney Parks are reachable after a 45-minute train ride from the heart of Paris if you are coming from there. Obtain a modest fare and board the clean RER train. Don't worry; you won't miss your stop because the final stop is in Marne-la-Vallée/Chessy, which is close to Disney Paris.

FastPass and tickets

Depending on the season, parks have different opening and closing hours for visitors. On the Disneyland Paris website, you can check the park hours for the day you intend to visit. You can also check here to see if your favorite rides and other attractions are open. There is an additional magic hour at the parks.

The cost of tickets at Disneyland is more expensive than the cost of tickets purchased online. To be on the safe side, always purchase your tickets online one day in advance.

When purchasing tickets, there are many options available. There is a chance that you will spend less if you get a multi-day ticket. You can use this to gain two days of unrestricted entrance to both the Walt Disney and Disneyland parks.

You can purchase a one-day ticket if you only want to ride your favorite rides and want to finish exploring the park in one day. You might be able to get the adult ticket for the price of the child ticket on a few days if this ticket has other incentives. You may also buy a day-dated shuttle ticket that entitles you to use the shuttle from Paris and admits you to the Disney Parks. In order to optimize your enjoyment of the park, you may also try the Fastpass, a sneaky system that enables you to skip the lines for the most popular attractions. Those having Disney Park admission tickets good for the same day are given the Fastpass, a little paper card, without charge. The distribution of Fastpasses is dependent on the availability of services and tickets. The wait time is definitely reduced greatly by using the Fastpass services, but you are not given priority access over other Fastpass users or guaranteed fast entrance to the ride. Fastpass is not accepted at private or special events at Disneyland Paris. To meet the demands of different tourists, there are multiple Fastpass options. I advise you to purchase the Unlimited-all-attractions Fastpass in order to enjoy yourself to the utmost.

Fastpass is only available for the rides mentioned below:

Big Thunder Mountain and Frontierland in Disneyland Park

- Discoveryland's Buzz Lightyear Laser Blast

Adventureland, Indiana Jones

- Fantasyland's Peter Pan's Flight

- Discoveryland and Star Tours: The Adventures Continue

- Discoveryland's Star Wars Hyperspace Mountain

Aerosmith-starring Rock 'n' Roller Coaster at Walt Disney Studios Park

- The Adventure of Ratatouille

- Toon Studio's Flying Carpets above Agrabah

Some of these attractions might not be open on the day the Fastpass is valid, and without warning Disneyland Paris may substitute another attraction of its choosing with a Fastpass lane in place of the unavailable one.

Amusements

After checking into our accommodations, let's take a stroll by and ride some of the attractions that make up the Disney Parks. For all age groups, Disneyland Paris has a lot to offer. There is no room or chance for anyone to be disappointed.

There are five magical areas in Disneyland Park: Main Street U.S., Fantasyland, Discovery Land, Frontierland, and Adventureland. And each of the 40 attractions is thoughtfully dispersed throughout these regions.

Fantasyland

Fantasyland is where the Disney Classics-themed attractions are located.

The renowned pink castle known as Le Château De La Belle Au Bois Dormant (Sleeping Beauty Castle) is a sight to behold. You may see various views of the park and the castle from various angles when strolling inside and outside the castle, respectively.

The Sleeping Beauty

The Sleeping Beauty Gallery, an attraction located inside the Sleeping Beauty Castle, uses antiques and other displays to illustrate the tale of the sleeping beauty.

La Tanière Du Dragon (The Dragon's Lair) is a straightforward amusement that features a strange maze beneath a castle and a dragon constructed of exquisite animatronic parts. The entire environment is set up to make children and a select group of adults anxious.

Peter Pan's Flight

One of the most well-liked rides, Peter Pan's Flight has one of the longest lines. You will set sail in a flying ship and experience the tale of Peter Pan on this gloomy storybook adventure. You should arrive early if you want to ride this because there are frequently long lines.

Alice in Wonderland

Similar to Alice, you can explore your own wonderland and navigate this hedge maze filled with Alice in Wonderland characters before reaching the Queen of Hearts' Castle. The views of Disneyland Paris from this castle are breathtaking.

Discovery Land

Discovery Land is the part of Disneyland Paris that is set in space. A must-do for any lover of Star Wars. The following is a list of this country's landmarks:

This ride, Star Wars Hyperspace Mountain (**Space Mountain Mission** 2), is a must-try for thrill-seekers and fans of the Star Wars franchise since it transports you on a space adventure. The ride is fascinating since it also features inversions.

Star Tours: The Adventures Continue (L'aventure Continue): This is a more contemporary version of the traditional simulator ship where you board and fly out into the Star Wars galaxy. Considering that there are

60 possible mission permutations, you can board this ride repeatedly.

An original walk-through exhibit of the Nautilus submarine from Jules Verne's books is called "The Mysteries of Nautilus." Even though it just takes five minutes to read through, if you stay longer, you might learn more valuable information.

Buzz Lightyear Laser Blast is a must-try if you enjoy shooting difficulties because it is a laser shooting ride.

Frontier land

Frontier land: A large area with stunning views that tells a cohesive story about the imagined city of Thunder Mesa. A handful of Frontier Land's attractions are listed below:

Big Thunder Mountain:

The most enjoyable and thrilling roller coaster is this one, which is softer in nature. Since this is one of the most popular rides, getting the best seats requires arriving early.

A replica of the Haunted Mansion is Phantom Manor. As soon as you look at it, it immediately strikes you as being creepier and spookier than its counterpart—the version from the magic land.

The Molly Brown riverboat, which will take you on a 20-minute journey, is available at the Thunder Mesa Riverboat Landing if you want to explore Frontierland's surroundings.

Adventure Land

This exotic place is built just for you if you're a fan of Pirates of the Caribbean, Indiana Jones, Aladdin, or Princess Jasmine. It is intricate yet lovely. Some attractions include:

Adventure Isle, the location of La Cabane des Robinson, is a perfect place to get lost because there is no way to be rescued there, not even by the map.

Based on the Indiana Jones films, it is an uncomfortable yet thrilling roller coaster ride. This fast train trip through the jungle is popular with children.

Pirates of the Caribbean: This creepy attraction may make it difficult to tell whether you are inside or outside after dusk.

This is a representation of Main Street U.S.A., which is mostly made up of stores and food stands. Its two galleries behind the stores in the Disneyland Paris version give it a distinctive feel.

Although they are not classified as attractions, Liberty Arcade and Discovery Arcade are must-visit locations to avoid the crowds. The tale of the Statue of Liberty is told at the Liberty Arcade. The 19th century's technical breakthrough is showcased at the Discovery Arcade.

The following attractions are located in Walt Disney Studios Park:
Ratatouille: The Journey: It's thrilling to see as you are miraculously reduced to the size of your favorite chef rat.

Take a tour of the legendary Hollywood Tower Hotel in the Tower of Terror. You board the eerie lift and descend 13 floors before entering the Twilight Zone.

RC Racer, Toy Story Parachute Drop, which lets you jump off the top of a parachute, and Slinky Dog Zigzag Spin, which lets you board a slinky dog and whisks you away on an exhilarating ride while the dog tries to catch his tail, are the other rides based on the Toy Story movie.

Drink and Food

At Disneyland Paris, food and drink are a bit pricey.

You have access to 68 food options at Disneyland Paris. 28 of them are in Disneyland Park, five are at Walt Disney Studios Park, seventeen are in Disney Village, and eighteen are near the hotels. Although the majority of them offer quick service, the remaining ones allow reservations both online and offline. Many eateries offer fast food options like pizza, burgers, Mexican food, and more. Both a la carte and a combo meal are available.

Among the notable dining establishments at Disneyland Paris are:
At Adventure Land, there is a cafe called Agrabah that serves an Arabic-inspired buffet. The Morocco Pavilion in Epcot may be seen in the design. Reservations advised.

Captain Jack's is a classy and cutting-edge restaurant that is located close to Pirates of the Caribbean on a ride.

Inventions: While dining here, you can engage with the familiar Disney characters.

L'Auberge de Cendrillon is comparable to Inventions but offers a menu rather than a buffet.

You are never required to purchase meals at Disneyland Paris; you are always welcome to bring your own. There are a lot of good bars there. In terms of Disneyland Paris, a decent pub crawl always incorporates food, which makes it an expensive crawl.

Each hotel offers a different selection of beers and cocktails. The cost varies between bars.

Last but not least, be wise and use the following advice while arranging a vacation to Disneyland Paris in order to have a good time:

To save time and avoid last-minute crowds and difficulties, make a list of the rides that each family member must experience.
To receive the best prices, reserve your hotels and tickets in advance.
Additionally, make reservations at restaurants in advance because they are sometimes overrun with large customers.

Instead of purchasing them at the parks, get costumes online to receive the best prices.

There is a lot of walking involved in the parks, so wear comfortable shoes to prevent fatigue.

Resorts

Six Disney hotels, including the Disneyland Hotel, Disney's Hotel Santa Fe, Disney's Sequoia Lodge, Disney's Hotel Cheyenne, Disney's Hotel New York, and Disney's Newport Bay Club, can be found in the expansive hotel section of Disneyland Paris. While the other two hotels, Disney's Davy Crockett's Ranch and Villages Nature Paris, are farther away from the park, all of these hotels are within 5–15 minutes of Disney Village, a small shopping district next to the park. You can leave your cottage and adventure imprints as soon as you step outdoors at Disney's Davy Crockett's Ranch. Additionally, the Aqua Lagoon, one of Europe's largest water parks, is one of five themed zones at the Villages Nature Paris resort, which is especially made for families. The cost per night ranges from 100 to 200 euros.

The cost of staying at the Disneyland hotel might change from €500 to €800 depending on the season, while the cost of Disney's Newport Bay Club could change from €200 to €400.

For Disney character fans, there is no better location to stay than a Disney hotel because you can get up close and personal with your favorite Disney characters there. But make sure to investigate this possibility before checking into the hotel.

Hotels outside of the Disney arena are more affordable than those close to the airport. Since the park is only a 10-minute train journey from the airport, choosing hotels near the airport is always more advantageous and practical for travelers.

Another option is to stay in Paris and travel to Disneyland for the day.

Visitors to Disneyland Paris are never disappointed. Therefore, although both parks may be seen in two days, it would be a wise choice to stay two nights and three days in order to have a comprehensive, in-depth understanding of the parks. Additionally, it takes little more than an hour and a half to fully visit Walt Disney World. Despite its high price, it is worthwhile to spend at least one night at the Disney resort.

You would have to go through security at each resort before leaving for the parks. The Disneyland Hotel might be an exception.

Since hotel costs are likely to fluctuate, it would be wise to research the deals and rates of the hotel before you check in. This could save you a lot of money that you might otherwise contemplate spending on other people or things.

In other words, it will be less expensive to book a package with Disney than to plan your travel arrangements separately.

Chapter 1

HISTORICAL HIGHLIGHTS: HISTORY AND CHRONOLOGY OF FRANCE

National identity has been a recurring theme throughout French history. As evidenced by fossil discoveries and cave paintings, France has been inhabited for a very long time. It was colonized by the Gauls, usurped by the Romans, and formed as a nation by the French. Before the storm clouds of revolution descended, the 17th and 18th centuries witnessed the rise and apogee of the monarchy as well as a golden age of study. Although it was necessary to topple the Ancien Régime, no one could agree on a new form of government. A century of constitutional experimentation followed. The fear of a "war to end all wars" replaced the Belle Epoque. France once more became the scene of an international conflict 20 years later. France had to overcome internal unrest to become a coherent country at ease with itself as it emerged from the misery of war. The problems of market liberalization, the environmental catastrophe, and addressing the requirements of a population that is becoming more diverse have all come with the 21st century.

• Historical chronology of France

France's Revolution
The events that are typically referred to as the French Revolution began in 1789, although they were actually a series of interconnected power battles. Louis XVI called a meeting of representatives chosen by the aristocracy, clergy, and Third Estate (the general public) to resolve the fiscal problem.

Country of Châteaux: the Loire valley
The Loire Valley is where France first became associated with elegance. After winning the Hundred Years War, French rulers were eager to flaunt their riches and their superiority over lower mortals. As strongholds, castles were no longer required, and lavish pleasure palaces started to appear in the valley's gentle, sensual terrain.

Beaches of D-day

The calm section of coast west of Cabourg, from Ouistreham to the Cotentin peninsula, was simply known as the Côte du Calvados before June 6, 1944. It was a flat, uninteresting beach punctuated by a few unremarkable chalk cliffs and sand dunes.

Study up on the D-day beaches.

Timeline of France
France in the prehistoric era (600 BC)

Marseille was founded by Greeks as Massalia.
58 BC

Under Julius Caesar, the Roman occupation of Gaul began.
3rd to 5th century AD

Franks, Vandals, and Goths invaded Roman Gaul as barbarians.

The Middle Ages in France 496

After driving the Romans out, Clovis the Frank, the first king of the Merovingian Dynasty, becomes a Christian.

751

Beginning the Carolingian dynasty is Pepin the Short.

800

Charlemagne, Pepin's son, is proclaimed Holy Roman Emperor.

843

The Carolingian Empire is broken into three by the Treaty of Verdun.

987

The Capetian Dynasty's first ruler is Hugh Capet.

1066

English invasion by the Normans.

1152

Eleanor of Aquitaine married Henry Plantagenet, who will become King Henry II of

England. English forces take control of one-third of France.
1305

Rome transfers the Papal See to Avignon.
1337

The Hundred Years' War officially began.

The Renaissance in France in 1415

Then, the battle of Agincourt was worn by Henry V. Of England
1429

At Orléans, Joan of Arc commands the French forces fighting the English. At Reims, Charles VII is crowned.
1431

At Rouen, Joan of Arc perished.
1453

The Hundred Year War is over.
1562-98

Religious conflicts pitted Catholics and Huguenots against one another.

1594

Henry of Navarre is crowned Henry IV after converting to Catholicism.

1624 France in the 17th and 18th centuries

In addition to suppressing Protestants, Cardinal Richelieu drags France into the Thirty Years' War.

1643

the coronation of "Sun King" Louis XIV.

1756-63

France loses her territories in North America during the Seven Years' War.

1769

Corsica being incorporated.

1778-1783

French assistance to the 13 colonies during the American Revolution.

1789

assault on the Bastille.

1792

Elimination of Louis XVI. The First Republic's proclamation.

1793

Louis XVI was put to death; Robespierre's Reign of Terror came to an end with his execution in 1794.

1804

Napoleon is crowned emperor and the Code is introduced. First Empire. Napoleon.

1815

The Battle of Waterloo results in Napoleon's defeat, and he is banished to St. Helena. 1830

Charles X is overthrown by revolution, and Louis-Philippe's July Monarchy takes his place.

1848

Deposed was Louis-Philippe, the Citizen King. Third Republic. 1851

Louis-Napoleon Bonaparte, Napoleon's nephew, carried out a coup d'état. Empire II. 1870

Napoleon III was overthrown as a result of the Franco-Prussian War. 1871

Paris Commune uprising that resulted in 25,000 fatalities. The Third Republic. 1889

The building of the Eiffel Tower; the Paris Universal Exposition. 1897-99

The Dreyfus Incident.

1914–18 in France in the 20th and 21st centuries

World War I was won by 1919's Versailles Peace Treaty.
1939

Starting point of World War II. 1940

Nazi soldiers invade and occupy France. 1944

On this day, the allies invaded Normandy on June 6th and Paris was freed.
1945

WWII's conclusion.
1946

Republic No. 4 is proclaimed. Indochina enters into war.
1954

The French leave Indochina. beginning of the Algerian uprising.
1958

The Fourth Republic is toppled by the Algerian crisis.
1959

The Fifth Republic's inaugural president was chosen by General de Gaulle.
1962

independence for Algeria.
1968

The de Gaulle administration is in danger of falling because of strikes and student unrest in Paris.
1981

President-elect François Mitterrand is chosen.
1995

President-elect Jacques Chirac is chosen.
2002

The euro is adopted as legal tender. Following a surprising victory for the Front National, Chirac is elected for a second term.
2007

With his campaign for strong changes, Nicolas Sarkozy prevails in the presidential race.
2012

President-elect François Hollande is a socialist.
2015

Over 140 people were killed in two distinct islamist terrorist assaults in Paris in January and November.
2016

Over 80 people were killed in a terrorist attack on Nice's promenade des Anglais.
2017

France elects Emmanuel Macron to lead the country.

Chapter 2

PLAN YOUR TRIP

Making Travel Plans to France

With Insight's travel tips on visas, embassies, transportation, healthcare, currency, and what to read, you can organize your trip to France.

- Entry requirements and visas

- Consulates and Embassies

- Travel

- Safety and health

- Budgeting and finances

- Reading material

Entry criteria and visas

To enter France, European citizens simply require a national identity card; however, individuals without one, such inhabitants of the UK and Ireland, must have a full passport. For stays of less than 90 days, visitors from Australia, Canada, New Zealand, and the USA must have a complete passport, although visas are not necessary. South African citizens traveling abroad need a passport and a visa. Before leaving on a trip, this must be obtained from the country's consulate.

Australia's embassies and consulates can be found at 4 rue Jean Rey, 75724 Paris, and online at http://france.embassy.gov.au.

Phone: 01 44 43 29 00; address: 35 avenue Montaigne, 75008 Paris; website: canadainternational.gc.ca/france

UK
75008 Paris; 18bis rue d'Anjou; 01 44 51 31 00; www.gov.uk/world/france

Paris, 75382; US 2 Avenue Gabriel; +1 43 12 22 22; website: https://fr.usembassy.gov

Transport

How to Reach France

By Air

Two airports serve Paris: All long-haul and the majority of international flights are handled by Roissy-Charles de Gaulle (CDG), which is 23 km (15 miles) northeast of the city; French domestic flights and some short-haul international flights are handled by Orly (ORY), which is 14 km (9 miles) south of the city center. tel: 3950 (or +33 1 70 36 39 50 if phoning from outside France; www.parisaeroport.fr) for information on both airports. There are numerous additional French airports that offer international flights, including Lyon, Bordeaux, Marseille, and Nice (tel: 08 20 42 33 33; www.nice.aeroport.fr).

The following airlines offer frequent flights from the UK to France: British Airways (www.britishairways.com), EasyJet (www.easyjet.com), Jet2 (www.jet2.com), and Ryanair (www.ryanair.com) are just a few of the airlines with websites.

Air France and the majority of national carriers offer direct flights from North America to Paris and other popular French cities like Nice and Lyon. Delta, United, and American Airlines all offer flights to France. From New York, Delta offers a daily trip to Nice.

By Sea

Between the UK, the Republic of Ireland, the Channel Islands, and France, a number of ferry services run many crossings every day, or at night for the longer sections. Most transport both automobiles and pedestrians. Prices vary from weekdays to weekends, depending on the season and the time of day. The major routes are Dover-Calais and Dover-Boulogne, which run alongside the Channel Tunnel and take 1½ to 1¼ hours. New services include Ramsgate-Boulogne and Ostend, and Dover-Dunkirk takes a bit longer but is less expensive. Although more expensive, the western Channel routes (to Dieppe, Le Havre, Caen, Cherbourg, St-Malo, or Roscoff) have longer and more luxurious crossings.

Brittany Ferries runs ferries between Portsmouth and Caen, Cherbourg and St. Malo, Poole to Cherbourg, Plymouth, and Cork to Roscoff (UK: 0871 244 0744; France: 08 25 82 88 28; www.brittanyferries.com). The average sailing time is 5 to 9 hours, but from April to October, fast catamarans go on the Cherbourg routes, averaging 2 to 3 hours.

Condor Ferries operates operations from Portsmouth-Cherbourg, Poole and Weymouth to St. Malo via Guernsey and Jersey (phone: 0845 609 1024; website: condorferries.co.uk).

High-speed catamaran ships travel four times daily (every 75 minutes) between Ramsgate and Boulogne by Euroferries (phone: 0844 414 5355; website: www.euroferries.com). In 2011, a Ramsgate-Ostend service was launched by Transeuropa Ferries (phone: 01843 595 522; website: transeuropaferry.com).

From Dover-Dunkirk, DFDSSeaways operates (phone: 0871 574 7235; website: www.dfdsseaways.co.uk). Some of the cheapest tickets are frequently found on the Dunkirk route (runs every two hours).

Up to 23 voyages each day between Dover and Calais are operated by P&O Ferries (UK: 0871 664 5645; France: 08 25 12 01 56; website: www.poferries.com). They also offer overnight trips between Hull and Zeebrugge.

There are 13 round departures every day between Dover and Calais offered by SeaFrance (UK: 0871 423 7119; France: 03 21 17 70 33; seafrance).

Portsmouth-Le Havre and Newhaven-Dieppe are two routes that are serviced by Transmanche Ferries/LD Lines (UK tel: 0844 576 8836; France tel: 08 25 30 43 04; transmanche-ferries).

Through rail About 20 High-speed Eurostar trains travel daily between London St. Pancras station and the Gare du Nord in Paris in 2 hours and 15 minutes, with certain trains also stopping at the Disneyland Paris Resort (UK: 08432 186 186; France: 08 92 35 35 39;

www.eurostar.com). When making a reservation, consider other periods because Eurostar fares fluctuate greatly depending on the season and time of day.

A hub of the French TGV high-speed rail system with direct services to various regions of the nation, Lille is where Eurostar trains also stop. Rail Europe (tel: 08448 484 064; website: https://en.oui.sncf) offers tickets that combine Eurostar and internal French trains.

By Car

The 35-minute Eurotunnel shuttle runs from Folkestone to Calais every day of the year, 24 hours a day, toll-free at 08443 35 35 35 in the UK and 0810 63 03 04 in France. The prices charged by Eurotunnel and the ferry providers differ significantly during peak and off-peak hours. The M20 highway in the UK and the A16 highway in France are connected via the tunnel.

Coach services are offered all throughout Europe by Eurolines (UK tel: 08717 818 181; France tel: 08 92 89 90 91; www.eurolines.de).

With fewer regular trips to other French cities, there are seven daily services between London Victoria coach station and Paris. This is among the least expensive methods of getting to France.

Moving About

Internal flights are only necessary for the longest distances within France because of the SNCF's (Société Nationale des Chemins de Fer) excellent rail system. The major towns and cities are connected by autoroutes; as they are primarily toll highways (péage), set aside money for them.

Domestic Flights

The majority of flights within France are operated by Air France, but it confronts fierce competition from low-cost carriers that now connect numerous regional airports in the UK.

Ferries Corsica Ferries run crossings from Toulon and Nice to Corsica (tel: +33 04 95 32 95 95; www.corsica-ferries.fr). From Toulon, Marseille, and Nice, SNCM (tel: 3260 if within France; www.sncf.com) ferries passengers to Corsica.

The ultra-comfortable high-speed trains known as TGVs (train à grande vitesse) are operated by Trains SNCF (tel. 3635; www.oui.sncf).

Corail Lunéa is a long-distance sleeper train, whilst Intercités and Téoz are more common express trains. Regional services called TER trains halt at every station.

All SNCF stations, as well as over the phone, online, and through Rail Europe, sell tickets. Always remember to confirm your ticket at the compostez votre billet machines before boarding.

Interstate Buses

Although less effective than rail, intercity bus services are frequently less expensive. Eurolines (see above) connects French cities. Ligne Express Régionale (LER; tel: 08 21 20 22 03; www.info-ler.fr) runs a vast network of buses throughout the Provence-Alpes-Côte d'Azur area.

Cycling

Ask at the nearby tourist information center about renting bicycles (vélos). In large towns and cities, public bicycle services like Vélo'V in Lyon are becoming more and more well-liked. At stations, bicycles can be rented and returned for a very cheap fee.

Driving

As long as you avoid traveling south on weekends throughout the summer, driving in France is a delightful experience. Weekends are ideal the rest of the year because HGVs are not allowed on highways. Since 2008, the road numbers have changed, and the majority of Route Nationale N highways are now D roads.

Traffic Situation

Since the government cracked down on speeding and drunk driving, road safety has increased. Be mindful that your speed can be estimated between toll booths when using an autoroute. The majority of French highways (autoroutes à péage) are tollways. On www.autoroutes.fr, information is offered in English, including a toll calculator.

Look for green holiday route signs (Bis) that indicate alternate routes because non-motorway main roads are frequently relatively empty (tel: 08 00 10 02 00 in French; www.bison-fute.gouv.fr).

Be aware that whereas gazole or gas-oil is diesel fuel, sans plomb is unleaded gasoline (gas).

Regulations

If you are detected disobeying the law, you may be subject to immediate fines and, in some cases, the confiscation of your driver's license. In case the police pull you over, be prepared with your driver's license, auto insurance, European vehicle recovery insurance, V5 vehicle registration certificate, European accident statement form, and passport.

• **Keep to the right.**

The legal limit for drunk driving in France is 0.5 milligrammes of alcohol per litre of blood.

• The following speed limits apply to toll roads: 130 kph (80 mph), urban dual carriageways 110 kph (68 mph), and outside of towns 90 kph (56 mph). Unless otherwise indicated, built-up areas are 50 kph (31 mph). When rainy, the restrictions are 10–20 kph lower.

Driving Organizations

Use the free emergency telephones located every two kilometers (1.14 miles) on highways or dial 17 to contact the police in an emergency. Having internationally recognised breakdown insurance is a good idea. Breakdown coverage is arranged by the insurance companies AA (tel: 0800 085 2753, 24-hour European Breakdown Helpline 00 800 88 77 66 55; www.theaa.com) and RAC (tel: 0800 015 6000; www.rac.co.uk).

Vehicle Rental

When purchasing your plane or train tickets, you can get greater prices on car rental than when you arrive in France. The age requirement to rent an automobile is 21. Some businesses won't rent to those who are over 60 or under 26. In most major cities, there are offices for all the main automobile rental firms, usually near the train station or airport.

Accessibility

Make sure you have all of your documentation with you since handicapped accessibility to public buildings has been improved, and parking is subject to the international blue system. Find worldwide dedicated parking places at www.bluebadgeparking.com.

A list of hotels with accessibility is published by the French tourism office, however individual amenities should be confirmed on site. Both the Michelin Red Guide for Hotels in France and the Michelin Green Guide for Camping and Caravanning in France have icons for accessible lodging. A free travel guide called Access in Paris is produced by Access Project (39 Bradley Gardens, West Ealing, London W13 8HE; www.accessinparis.org), and Tourism for All (tel: 0845 124 9971; www.tourismforall.org.uk) offers in-depth travel information.

Safety and Health

An EHIC Card
The French state health service (Sécurité Sociale) offers some of the greatest medical treatment available anywhere in the world. The fundamental distinction between the French state system and the National Health Service of the UK is that in the former, you must pay for all medical care and prescription drugs up front before claiming a reimbursement, sometimes for the full amount or at least 70%. You must be

an EU citizen and in possession of an EHIC in order to be eligible for this. The NHS (tel: 0845 606 2030; www.nhs.uk) offers free EHIC applications by the mail, telephone, and internet. A brochure that details the protocols to be followed in each nation is included with the EHIC.

In order to be eligible for reimbursement of medical expenses through the EHIC, you must only use the public health system—not a private facility—and, if at all feasible, show your card right away. The EHIC will be adequate for the majority of circumstances and initial emergency care, but you should be aware that it does not cover all costs or all possibilities, including the cost of repatriation in the event of a serious accident. It is therefore crucial to purchase private travel insurance.

You must keep the feuille de soins, or treatment form, from the doctor or hospital as well as the stickers from the prescription pill packets in order to claim the cost of medical expenses. Before you depart for home, follow the guidelines on your EHIC to recoup around 80%

of the expenses from the Caisse Primaire d'Assurance Maladie (CPAM), the neighbourhood health centre where you are staying. If you require additional assistance, get in touch with the Centre des Liaisons Européennes et Internationales de Sécurité Sociale (CLEISS; tel: 01 45 26 33 41; www.cleiss.fr). This can take some time, so if you can't get paid before you go, get in touch with the Department for Work & Pensions upon your return (UK tel: 0191 218 1999).

If you visit a doctor, budget between €21 and €25 for a straightforward consultation plus any medication costs.

Emergency situations and health insurance
All cities and towns have hospitals with general casualty/emergency departments (urgences), or you can call the SAMU ambulance service (see right) if you have a medical emergency. For information about English-speaking medical professionals in each location, consult consulates (and frequently hotels) (see fact boxes at the beginning of chapters for hospitals in your area).

Visitors from outside the EU should have comprehensive private travel and medical insurance. If they experience a medical emergency, they can use either private or public facilities, retain the same records as EU citizens, and then file a claim with their insurance for reimbursement. IAMAT is a specialized travel health service that offers insurance and a database of English-speaking physicians worldwide (USA: 1-716-754 4883; Canada: 1-416-652 0137; www.iamat.org).

Pharmacies

There are many pharmacies in French towns, and they can be recognised by a green cross sign that is illuminated at night. Since French chemists have substantial training, it will be simpler to see a chemist regarding minor ailments, bites, and other issues rather than seeking medical attention. A card in each drugstore's window lists the address of the closest duty pharmacy (pharmacie de garde) that is open after regular business hours and on Sundays.

Budgeting For Your Trip And Money

Currency

The euro (€), the official currency of France, is available in denominations of 500, 200, 100, 50, 20, 10, 5, and 5 euro notes as well as 2, 1, 50, 20, 10, 5, 2, and 1 euro coins. One euro is equal to 100 cents. Exchange rates at the time of publication were 1 euro = 88 pence or $1.44. You must declare any foreign currency you bring into or take out of France that is valued at least €10,000.

Cards and Cash

In France, popular credit and debit cards including Visa, MasterCard, and Maestro are widely used. The simplest way to exchange money is by using your card at an ATM, however this can be expensive, so it is best to compare rates before you travel. Using a debit card to make an ATM withdrawal used to be more cost-effective, but now days it's advisable to get a credit card with a decent offer. As an alternative, you might obtain a prepaid credit card and load your vacation funds onto it before you depart, but there might still be an ATM fee.

Cards are referred to as cartes bancaires in French; a sign with the letters CB indicates that credit cards are accepted. Make sure you have alternate payment methods on hand because automatic toll payment devices at many petrol stations and on highways don't always accept international credit cards. Before using a card overseas, it is advisable to let your bank or other card issuer know to prevent the card from having security barred.

The chip-and-pin mechanism used by cards in France is identical to that used in the UK (the French word for PIN is code personal). Additional ID may be required if you pay with a card. You will need to request that your card be swiped if you have a US or Canadian card that isn't yet chip-and-pin coded. Particularly in Paris, most waiters and store employees are accustomed to this.

Be aware that there is a cash withdrawal fee when using a credit card or some debit cards at a Bureau de Change; you will also need to show your passport when changing money. Avoid purchasing cash at ferry docks and airports since they provide the poorest exchange rates; you can obtain a better rate by ordering up to four hours in advance. Hotel commission rates are always high.

Banks have exchange (change) counters and are typically open Monday through Friday from 10 a.m. to 5 p.m. in cities. Banks are open from Tuesday through Saturday from 10 a.m. to 1 p.m. to 5 p.m., closing early the day before a holiday.

Traveler's checks are less popular these days because ATMs are so widely available. Although not all banks would cash them, some hotels will accept them as payment. You can have trouble finding a place to cash traveler's checks in isolated rural places.

Tipping

Service fees are typically included in restaurant bills (service compris). If the waiter's service was especially good, it's customary to leave a tiny extra tip. Tipping hotel chambermaids €1.50 per day and taxi drivers 10% are typical.

Tax

The standard rate of tax, or TVA, on sales and services is 19.5 percent, while the reduced rate is 5.5 percent. Both rates are always included in the price indicated at the appropriate rate. Depending on the kind of lodging, a tourism tax that is levied on accommodations is assessed at rates specified by the local government and can range from €0.20 to €1.50 per person per day.

Chapter 3

BEST TIME OF YEAR TO VISIT

Nowadays, many communities host summertime events that are open to both residents and visitors. You can be invited to take part in neighborhood celebrations if you are staying on a farm or in a rural location. Almost every town and village hosts a festival during the summer, with events ranging from straightforward boules tournaments with a dance to elaborate carnivals complete with street theater, fireworks, and high-brow entertainment, all hosted by enthusiastic (and occasionally agonizing) bands playing traditional music.

France's Weather

The majority of the north of France experiences a variable and seasonal climate that is generally temperate with mild summer temperatures, soggy autumns, early springs, and frigid winters. While the climate in southern Brittany and the Loire Valley is milder and significantly warmer, there may occasionally be strong storms along the Atlantic coast, especially in northern Brittany and the Cotentin Peninsula of Normandy.

There are always significant temperature fluctuations between low and high altitudes in the east, which includes the Alps and the Massif Central. The east also tends to have pleasant summers and cold, snowy winters. The Mediterranean coast experiences extremely hot, dry summers and mild, showery winters; when they blow, powerful winds can be inconvenient. With the exception of this coast, rainfall is irregular year-round, occurring most frequently between January and April and least frequently between July and August; the wettest place in France is Mont Aigoual in the Cévennes National Park.

Paris has generally pleasant weather, especially in the spring; summer is frequently hot, autumn is moderate, and winter is tolerable, though there has been snow in the city in recent years.

France's High And Low Seasons

Any time of year is a terrific opportunity to travel to France. The south is best avoided in August, though, as that is when the French enjoy their annual vacation and traffic may be quite congested.

In August, many businesses in Paris lock their doors, but this calm time might be a fantastic opportunity to explore the city because hotel costs are typically lower.

Mid-June to mid-September is high season in well-traveled locations; July and August are high seasons elsewhere. Mid-December to mid-May are the ski resorts' operating dates; however, skipping the British and French school holidays will save you money and prevent long lift lines and congested mountain routes.

France's Events and Festivals

The major annual events are briefly described here, but there are hundreds more happening in the smaller towns and villages. You can search events in France by month, location, and category on www.viafrance.com and www.culture.fr, or you can get more detailed information by getting in touch with the neighborhood tourist offices.

January
Varying La Grande Odyssée dates
Haute Savoie and Savoie

One of the toughest dog sled races in the world attracts mushers to the Alps. For dates, visit www.grandeodyssee.com.

Varying La Folle Journée dates in February
Nantes

The biggest classical music event in France honors a different composer every year. Each music concert lasts no more than 45 minutes and is held in an unconventional setting. For exact dates, visit www.follejournee.fr.

Nice several dates for the funfair

This, one of the biggest carnivals in the world, has been going on since at least 1294. Every year, more than a million tourists arrive in the city for two weeks of frolicking entertainment. For exact dates, visit www.nicecarnaval.com

Dates for the April International Kite Festival vary.
Pas-de-Calais' Berck-sur-Mer

Europe's largest kite-flying festival is held every year in this family-friendly resort in northern France. Kite aficionados from all over the world attend. For exact dates, visit www.cerf-volant-berck.com.

Ouest-France Spi Regatta dates can vary.
Trinité-sur-Mer, La

400 yachts arrive at this scenic port in southern Brittany for the biggest yacht gathering in Europe and a week of racing. For exact dates, see www.spi-ouestfrance.com.

The dates of the Cannes Film Festival can change.

In one of the most hideous structures on the Côte d'Azur, this upscale yet endearing beach town presents the glitziest film festival in the entire world. Almost certainly catch a glimpse of an A-lister. For exact dates, visit www.festival-cannes.fr.

Paris typically hosts the French Open Tennis Tournament from the last week of May to the first week of June.

To win this coveted Grand Slam title, top tennis players compete on the clay courts at Roland Garros. For exact dates, visit www.rolandgarros.com.

Dates for the June Feria de Nîmes varied Nîmes

In the spectacular Roman arena of Nîmes, there were five days of bullfighting and coarse camarguaises (non-mortal bull baiting). The atmosphere and street celebrations attract the majority of visitors. For exact dates, visit www.ot-nimes.fr.

Dates for Rendez-Vous aux Jardins (Garden Open Days) can vary

Over the course of three days, guests can take guided tours of some of France's greatest public and private gardens. Every year has a distinct theme. For exact dates, visit www.rendezvousauxjardins.culture.fr

Avignon Festival dates in July change Avignon

In one of France's most picturesque cities, the most significant theater festival is held. For exact dates, see www.festival-avignon.com.

14th of July Paris/National

The French Revolution begins with a grand military parade in Paris, but everyone in France celebrates.

Variable dates for the Lorraine Hot Air Balloon Festival Chambley-Bussières

Over the course of ten days, the biggest hot air balloon festival in the world draws more than 400,000 spectators and about 3,000 pilots. For exact dates, visit www.pilatre-de-rozier.com.

Dates for the Tour de France varied National

This yearly, three-week long, international cycle competition includes challenging Alpine climbs and covers over 3,600km (2,200 miles) in roughly 20 stages. For exact dates, visit www.letour.fr.

Various dates for the August Celtic Festival Lorient

The town, which also happens to be France's second-largest fishing port, celebrates Europe's Celtic cultures for seven days through music, art, literature, and dance. For exact dates, visit http://festival-interceltique.com.

Third weekend of September is National September Heritage Days.

On the third weekend in September, important public and private structures for art or architecture welcome visitors.

Strasbourg Christmas Market from the end of November to the end of December

The oldest Christmas market in France is situated in the charming old town of the city. Little ones will be delighted with the Children's Village. For additional information, visit www.noel.strasbourg.eu.

8th Lyon Fête des Lumières

During the Festival of Lights, the Virgin Mary is honored with a candlelit procession, illuminated buildings, and creative light shows. According to legend, she ward off the plague in

Lyon in 1643. To learn more, visit www.fetedeslumieres.lyon.fr

Chapter 4

FRANCE'S TOP RESTAURANTS

There are many fantastic restaurants in France, from the elegant classics to the small inns that may only have one menu of locally produced food.

The famous confits of duck and goose in the southwest, the choucroute (sauerkraut) in the east, the coq au vin (chicken in red wine sauce) in Burgundy, and the fantastic seafood all along the coast are just a few of the regional specialties.

France offers great value for money while dining out, and it is still uncommon to have a terrible meal—except on rare occasions in Paris or along the Côte d'Azur. It is usually worthwhile to try the local cuisine because it is likely to be the freshest and most expertly prepared, and it is the finest way to experience a region's flavour when paired with local wine. These days, regional French cooking is trendy, and many of Paris' most well-known eateries specialise on regional cuisine. There aren't many vegetarian options available in France because the trend hasn't really taken hold yet.

France's best restaurants
3 Rue des Chats Bossus, A l'Huîtrière, 03 20 55 43 41, http://www.huitriere.fr

One of the top restaurants in the city, providing seafood and other classic meals in a gorgeous tiled Art Deco setting in Lille's historic district. Outstanding wine list. The day before a few holidays and in August are closed.

5 rue de la Gare, Au Cerf, 67250 Hunspach
03 88 80 41 59, www.aucerf.fr.

The ideal place to eat when visiting one of Alsace's most picturesque villages is in the northern Vosges. A feuilleté of regional Munster cheese and choucroute with fish are two dishes on the menu.

Les Crayères 64 Boulevard Henry Vasnier, Reims, France, 326-24-90-00
www.lescrayeres.com

Haute cuisine served in an opulent château hotel with an outstanding choice of vintage champagnes to pair with the gourmet fare. Le Jardin brasserie (€€), located in the lovely garden of the château, is another little more affordable, less formal, but no less appealing alternative. Closed on Monday and Tuesday.

Etang de Diane, Aux Coquillages de Diana, 20270 Aléria 04 95 57 04 55
www.auxcoquillagesdediana.fr

a floating eatery that serves fish, oysters, and mussels from the lake of Aléria on the island of Corsica's east coast. Great patio with oyster beds in the background. Evening closure Oct. 1-May. 10, and all of January.

Bayonne, New Jersey 64100 Auberge du Cheval Blanc, 68 rue Bourgneuf
05 59 59 01 33

The current chef, Jean-Claude Tellechea, has earned a Michelin star for his work at this venerable Petit Bayonne establishment that has been serving traditional Basque food for more than 50 years. Sat. at noon, Sun. at sunset, and Mon.

The Corps of Guard at the third level of Notre Dame, 35400 St. Malo, (02) 994-094-06, www.le-corps-de-garde.com.

This affordable creperie offers a unique feature because it is the only eatery located on the walls of old St. Malo. As a result, you can enjoy mouthwatering sea views while indulging on crêpes or savoury galettes.

Dijon, France 21000 Le Pré aux Clercs 13 Place de la Libération 03 80 38 05 05, www.jeanpierrebilloux.com.

Father-and-son combination Jean-Pierre and Alexis Billoux prepare delectable traditional Burgundian food with panache and accompany it with premium wines. The more affordable Bistrot des Halles (€-€€) and Brasserie Bg (€) are nearby. Sun evening and Mon are closed.

Strasbourg, France 03 88 32 42 14 Maison Kammerzell 16 Place de la Cathédrale

www.maison-kammerzell.com

Excellent cuisine and drink are served in one of Strasbourg's oldest homes, close to the cathedral. The Renaissance-era building's frescoed interior serves as a fitting background to the superb renditions of Alsatian cuisine, including the region's characteristic choucroute with three different fish.

68 34 21 84 Casa Sansa 2 rue Fabriques d'en Nadal, 66000 Perpignan, www.casa-sansa.fr.

Locals love the lively Catalan eatery in the old town, which serves mouthwatering fare including grilled squid, suquet (fish stew), and chargrilled lamb.

03 86 33 39 10 L'Espérance 89450 Saint-Père-en-Vézelay

www.marc-meneau-esperance.com

Marc Meneau's renowned hotel-restaurant offers a lavish experience with an opulent conservatory dining room, outstanding food based on traditional Burgundy ingredients, and a wine cellar to match. Mon, Tue, Wed, and Jan-Feb are all closed at noon.

L'Esplanade, 24250 Domme, Rue Carral

05 53 28 31 41

www.esplanade-perigord.com

This welcoming, family-run hotel-restaurant is positioned above the River Domme and offers stunning views of the Dordogne Valley. Each spring, a variety of dishes using truffles are served as part of the superb local cuisine. Mid-November through mid-January closed.

Bordeaux: 5 rue Montesquieu, 33000 Le Chapon Fin, 05 56 79 10 10.

www.chapon-fin.com

Visit this Art Nouveau-inspired Bordeaux restaurant to experience excellent service and upscale regional cuisine like langoustines with caviar and sea bass with forest mushrooms. Sun and Mon are closed.

Café de la Fontaine is located at 4 General de Gaulle Avenue in La Turbie.
04 93 28 52 79
www.hostelleriejerome.com

The village café has been expertly transformed by Bruno Cirino of the Hostellerie Jérôme into a relaxed but stylish restaurant with a fantastically affordable blackboard menu of homely specialties, including rabbit cooked in the manner of Nice and homemade fruit tarts. open for both lunch and dinner. Winter Mondays are closed.

Place du Casino
Le Café de Paris
377-98 06 76 23

One of the must-see attractions in Monte-Carlo is the completely restored, 1920s-style location where Edward VII allegedly invented the crêpe Suzette by accident (and gave it his mistress' name). Food from a traditional brasserie and excellent people-watching from the terrace.

7300 Chambéry L'Essentiel
183 place de la Gare
04 79 96 97 27

One of the greatest in Savoie, known for its excellent preparation of alpine specialties. Sun and Mon at noon are closed.

29550 Ste-Anne-la-Palud,
Hotel de la Plage
02 98 92 50 12
www.plage.com

Gourmet seafood and other delectable delicacies are served in a stunning setting above the beach in a small village near Douarnenez, with a spectacular view across the waters. A deluxe hotel as well. Nov. – Mar. closed.

Arras, France La Faisanderie
45 Grand'Place
03 21 48 20 76
www.restaurant-la-faisanderie.com

This charming restaurant is located in one of the Boves cellars beneath Arras' Grand Place and has the ambiance of a cosy haven away from the bustle of the city. Local ingredients are expertly incorporated into seasonal dishes that are refined, and the wine list is excellent.

Rouen 02 35 71 86 07
Brasserie Paul
1 place de la Cathédrale
www.brasserie-paul.com

Numerous notable citizens of Rouen, including Simone de Beauvoir and Marcel Duchamp, frequented this venerable brasserie. There is something on the menu for everyone, and it is directly across from the church.

Place de l'Eglise,
19500 Collonges-la-Rouge,
Auberge Le Prieuré
05 55 25 41 00
www.le-prieure.fr

A charming traditional inn offering delicious regional cuisine in the heart of this historic Corrèze town, as well as a picturesque patio for fine weather. Wednesdays are closed from September to May.

42 Rue Rabelais,
L'Ardoise, 37500 Chinon,
02 47 58 48 78
www.lardoise-chinon.com

Chef Stéphane Perrot creates high-quality dishes in his restaurant in the heart of Chinon, like a millefeuille of salmon and langoustines.

35 street Saint Jean du Pérot, L'Entracte,
17000 La Rochelle
05 46 52 26 69
www.lentracte.net

One of three establishments in La Rochelle established by renowned chef Grégory Coutanceau that serves more conventional French dishes. Le Comptoir des Voyages features more internationally inspired food, while Les Flots offers more experimental fare.

3 rue Lafayette,
Toulouse, 31000;
 La Bohème
05 61 23 24 18
www.la-boheme-toulouse.com

A charming eatery serving cassoulet, magret aux cèpes, and other traditional Toulouse fare in a domed cellar close to Place du Capitole. Sat. at noon and Sun.

10 Quai de la Quarantaine,
14600 Honfleur,
France 02 31 89 39 00 L'Absinthe
www.absinthe.fr

A wonderful restaurant in the historic district of Honfleur with a charming quayside terrace, first-rate service, and inventive modern cuisine. The proprietors also run a lovely hotel.

01 42 74 57 81,
404 69 rue des Gravilliers,
http://404-resto.com/restaurant/paris/404

crowded, cool, and atmospheric with low seating and iron window grilles that reflect lacy patterns onto the tables through the dim interior. The Moroccan menu offers fragrant Berber desserts, lamb brochettes, unusual couscous and tagines, and filo-pastry pies. Quite decent food for the price. Booking is necessary.

13 rue des Beaux-Arts,
 St. Germain-des-Prés,
 6th 01 44 41 99 00
Le Restaurant - L'Hôtel, www.l-hotel.com.

Oscar Wilde's famous hotel, where he passed away in 1900, has undergone a spectacular boutique renovation, and its Michelin-starred restaurant serves up creative modern cuisine.

17 rue de Beaujolais,
Le Grand Véfour Jardins du Palais-Royal, 1st 01 42 96 56 27
www.grand-vefour.com

One of the oldest eateries in the city, open since 1784. The dining area is excellent, and chef Guy Martin's food is delectable for gourmets. Sat., Sun., and Aug. are closed.

Avenue Tour Eiffel,
 7th 01 45 55 61 44
Jules Verne Tour Eiffel
www.lejulesverne-paris.com

This is the most remarkable of the three restaurants on the Eiffel Tower, featuring an ambitious Alain Ducasse menu and breathtaking views from the second level. On level 1, 58 Tour Eiffel (phone: 08 25 56 66 62; €) is a close second.
St. Germain-des-Prés,
France Le Comptoir Hôtel Relais Saint-Germain 9 Carrefour de l'Odéon 6th 01 44 27 07 97
www.hotel-paris-relais-saint-germain.com

With this contemporary bistro's light, inventive takes on traditional fare at affordable rates, chef Yves Camdeborde has had a significant impact. It is a component of his stylish hotel, which also boasts a bar with enticing appetizers.

55 rue Traversière,
12th L'Encrier
01 44 68 08 16

It has all the qualities you hope for in a restaurant: great prices, traditional decor, an open kitchen, a lively local clientele, friendly staff, and decent bistro fare like, say, fried rabbit kidneys on salad with raspberry vinegar or homemade terrine or goose magret (breast) with honey. Lastly, serve profiteroles.

Jacques Gagnaire
6 rue Balzac, 01 58 36 12 50,
Hotel,Balzac. www.pierre-gagnaire.com.

One of the most inventive and creative chefs working today is Pierre Gagnaire. Consider suckling lamb rubbed in ewe's milk curd and capers served with roasted rice, Chinese cabbage with toasted rice, and snails with fennel shoots for examples of his complex composition, which borders on the baroque. Intrepid diners must make a stop in this subdued gray dining space. Always make reservations ahead of time before traveling.

32 Rue St. Marc in Aux Lyonnais located at (842)
96 65 04, www.auxlyonnais.com.

This 1892-established cafe has been tastefully updated by Alain Ducasse while retaining its original design. The menu features pike, perch, and crayfish quenelles as homages to Lyonnaise specialties. Frog legs from Dombes, charcuterie, top-notch meat cuts, and local wines. Reserve far in advance.

106 rue de la Folie-Méricourt,
11th 01
43 57 33 78,
Auberge Pyrénées-Cévennes

This upscale restaurant just earned a best bistro award for a reason: the waitstaff is helpful, the design is distinctive (terracotta floors, purple-and-white tablecloths, and, weirdly enough, a few stuffed animal heads on the wall), and the hearty food is excellent. Start with lentil caviar or a frisée aux lardons (bacon salad) then move on to cassoulet, pigs' feet, sausage and potatoes, salmon quenelles, rum Babas or profiteroles for your main course.

11 rue Neuve 04
 78 28 62 91 La Meunière
www.la-meuniere.fr

One of the most iconic bouchons lyonnais, or traditional inns, where patrons may enjoy the city's renownedly bountiful cuisine—meaty salads, several aperitifs, amazing cheeses, and rich wines—in a warm and welcoming setting. Closed Sun and Mon.

Corniche Le Péron
56 Kennedy, J.F.

04 91 59 25 92
www.restaurant-peron.com

A chic, modern restaurant with breathtaking ocean views. Cooking is skillful and creative. hotspot in Marseille.

53 Cours Mirabeau, Les Deux Garçons
Churchill, Colette, and Cézanne are just a few of the notable people that have visited Les Deux Garçons. Founded in 1792, this centre of knowledge includes a charming patio for people-watching and a brasserie-style dining room with decor from the Consular era.

Top Cafebars France's Best Cafes And Bars

French cafés are a cultural institution where people go to see and be seen. Order a café-crème, take a seat, and observe the world -- and its canine -- passing by.

French cafes and pubs to visit

19 rue des Fossés-Saint-Jacques,
01 44 07 04 41
 Café de la Nouvelle Mairie
This laid-back Latin Quarter bar offers an excellent selection of minor French producers' wines by the glass or bottle. The Massif Central offers delectable Aveyron cuisine for dining. Sun closed.

9th Place de l'Opéra,
Café de la Paix
 01 40 07 36 36
This lovely café/brasserie with Charles Garnier decor is listed as a historic monument; the terrace is an excellent place to people-watch.

01 43 54 31 61, Berthillon 29-31 rue Saint-Louis-en-l'Ile,
The ice cream treats created in this renowned ice cream parlor on the Ile St-Louis are a staple of Parisian culture. Purchase them to take home or consume them in the salon de thé with coffee and pastries.

100 rue Saint-Martin,

01 48 87 63 96,
Café Beaubourg
A favorite destination for locals and visitors alike, the fashionably chic café next to the Centre Pompidou has a large terrace and a menu that features light, cosmopolitan meals.

93 rue de Rivoli,
01 49 26 06 60
Café Marly
The most upscale location in the vicinity of the Louvre for coffee, a beverage, or lunch, with an arcaded terrace facing the pyramid. the perfect place to unwind after seeing the galleries.

Chapter 5

USEFUL PHRASES: French Expressions and Pronunciations to Use.

Worldwide, there are 129 million native French speakers. One of the five official languages of the United Nations, French (français) is recognised as the official language in 30 nations. It is a Romance language, like Italian and Spanish, descended from Vulgar Latin, and is spoken by 1.3 million people in Switzerland, 4 million in Belgium, 7 million in Canada (mostly Quebec), 60.5 million in France, and 7 million in Italy. 22 African countries have it as their official language.

- Typical

- Figures

- Entrance and exit

Cash and banking

- Travel

The provision of

- Emergencies.

- Wellness

Dining out

General

Describe yourself. How do you refer to yourself?

My name is... I go by...

Are you an English speaker? Do you speak English?

I am an English/American, I am an English/American.

I don't comprehend I don't understand

Please speak more slowly. "Speak more slowly," I beg you.

Can you assist me? Can you assist me?

I'm looking for... I'm searching for

What is it? Où est...?

Sorry, excuse me/excuse me

I'm unsure Je ne sais pas

Enjoy your day! Good morning!

That's it, that's it.

This is itVoici

Voilà, there it is.

Onward we go On y va. Allons-y

I'll see you then, bye.

As soon as possible

Show me the word in the book Show me the word in the book

Yes, sir

no non

Please, if you would

Thank you, please

(very) (plenty)

Your welcome, nothing at all

Excuse me, please.

hey good day

Okay, I agree.

goodbye and good bye

Good night, bonsoir

this ici

Then there

currently today

last day here

tomorrow december

Now that you've

later than usual

early this morning

This afternoon, this afternoon

presently ce soir

Hours of the Day
Monday, Monday

Dienstag mardi

Wednesday, Wednesday

Friday, Thursday

Friday, Friday

Date: Saturday

Sunday, Sunday

Seasons
Spring is in the air.

a summer's day

l'automne, fall

Winter is here.

Months
January is January

February, February

Mars in March

Month of April

May I,

July June

July is July.

August, August

the month of September

Month of October

The month of November

November December

Numbers
0 zéro

1 un, une

2 deux

3 trois

Four four

5 cinq

6 six

7 sept

8 huit

9 neuf

10 dix

11 onze

12 douze

13 triples

14 quarters

15 fives

16 seize

17 September

18 ten-eight

A 19-dix-neuf

20 vingt

21 Twenty-One

30 thirty

40 quatre

50 fifty-nine

60 plus 20

70 sixty-five

80 quadruplets

90 four vein-dix

100 cent

1,000 mille

One billion zero million

Arriving and Leaving

I would like to exit at... Je voudrais descendre à...

Which avenue is this? Where in the street are we?

What queue should I take for...? What path should I take to...?

How far is that? What distance is it from there?

Validate your ticket by typing your ticket.

airline terminal

station for trains la gare

La Gare Routière, a bus terminal

Métro stop at the Métro station

bus the bus, drive a car

bus l'arrêt stop

station le quai

le billet du ticket

aller-retour for a return journey

Hitting the roadside

toilets, the restrooms

The hotel address is as follows: C'est l'adresse de l'hôtel

I would like a (single/double) room. I would prefer a (single/double) room.

...with shower and toilet

...with a bath with a bathroom

with a view, with a view

Does breakfast go under that? Is breakfast included?

Can I come into the room? Can I see the bedroom?

wash basin / toilet

bed, light

keyla clef

lift/elevator operator

Conditioned by air conditioning

pool swimming la piscine

to make a reservation

Banking and money
Where's...?

Où est...?

the ATM

- the automatic distribution of tickets

The bank.

The Bank

- the exchange bureau for currencies

- The change bureau

When is the bank open and shut?

When does the bank open or close?

I want to convert dollars or pounds into euros.

I want to convert pounds sterling and dollars to euros.

Transport

How can I go to the city?

How will I get around town?

Where's...?

Où est...?

- an airport.

- the airport

- the railway (train) station

the gate

- the bus terminal

- the railway station

- the subway [underground] station

the underground

How far is it from here?

It's not today, is it?

How can I purchase a ticket?

Where can I purchase a ticket?

a single round-trip or one-way journey ticket for...

A simple ticket for an aller-retour...

The amount?

What does it cost?

Which queue or gate?

What door or queue?

On what platform?

What is it?

How can I find a taxi?

Where can I find a taxi?

Bring me to this location.

Please lead me to this address.

Please provide me a map.

Do I have access to a card?

Accommodation
Could you suggest a hotel?

Could you suggest a hotel to me?

I reserved a spot.

I made a reservation.

Who am I?

My name is

Have you have a room…?

Do you have a room?

for one or two

- for one or two

containing a bathroom

- with bathroom.

featuring air conditioning

- with climate control

For ...

Pour...

this evening

This evening

2-night period

- 2 nights

- a week.

an entire week

The amount?

What does it cost?

Is there a less expensive option?

Is there anything cheaper than this?

When can I leave?

When do I need to leave the bedroom?

I'll pay cash or using a credit card.

I'll pay in cash or with a credit card.

Please give me my bill or a receipt.

Can I have my invoice or a receipt?

Emergencies

Help! Au revoir!

Stop! Arrêtez!

Call a physician Dial un médecin

Dial 911 or Appelez une ambulance

Make a police call Dial la police

The fire department should be contacted.

Where is the closest phone located? Where is the closest phone number?

Which hospital is the closest to me? The closest hospital is where?

I'm ill I'm sick I'm sick

J'ai perdu mon passeport/porte-monnaie I've misplaced my purse

Health

I'm sick [unwell].

I'm not well.

I require a physician who speaks English.

I need a doctor who speaks English.

Here, it hurts.

It is bad here.

I'm hurting.

I'm bad.

Where is the pharmacy/chemist?

Where is the pharmacy?

When does it open and close?

What time does it open and close?

I have an allergy to

I have an allergy to...

Dining out

breakfast The morning meal

lunch and breakfast

Le dîner, or dinner

meal the meal

first course the entrée/the appetiser

major course, the main dish

puddings and other sweets

veggies, vegetables

the fruit fruit

beverage includes boisson included

wine list the wine list

a fork and knife

sword le couteau

spoon the needle

plate with a spoon

Glass is glass.

serviette, serving spoon

l'addition bill

I eat vegetarian food I am a vegetarian

I'm on a diet I'm on a regimen

What do you suggest? Which would you recommend?

Do you offer any regional specialties? Have you got any regional specialties?

I want to make a purchase Je voudrais commander

That is not what I ordered. That is not what I ordered.

Service is it included?   Has the service been completed?

Cheers! Enjoy your lunch!

Snacks and Breakfast
hurt bread

butter, beurre

pepper flakes

salt sel

sulphate sugar

jam confiture

Eggs oeufs

Pudding soup

Viande La - Meat
very rare blue

rare and savage

au point moyen

Bien cuit Congratulations!

Grillé cooked

lamb from agneau

steak bifteck

Cattle Duck

bulgari stuffed

hambon jambon

rabbit lapin

poultry breast

young poussin chicken

kidneys of Roger

Venison Veal

Fish Poissons
ahi anchovies

loup or bar sea bass

barbecued well

cod cabillaud

tranquil squid

shellfish coquillage

crevette prawns

sea bream with daubing

Halibut flotan

herring hareng

lobster homard

oyster huître

Lemon sole (limande)

monkfish lotte

skater in raie

salmon steaks

tuna thon

Trout, rainbow

the Café
consumes less alcohol

coffee shop

...with milk, cream au lait, or cream

...decaféiné déca/décaféinated

...express, espresso noir, and black

...American-style coffee filters

tea thé

Herbal tisane infusion

...camomile tincture

piping hot chocolate chaud

a milkshake

entire full cream

... semi-skimmed demi-crémé

... skimmed the paper

eau minérale, a mineral water

dazzling, still, or not gazing

Served with sugar and citron pressé, fresh lemon juice

Orange pressée juice freshly squeezed

either cool or fresh frais, fraîche

bière (beer)

bottled in a bottle

...on tap at pressure

Cassis (blackcurrant liqueur) and white wine

kir royale made with champagne

avec des glaçons, ice

nice second

Red rooster

the colour white

Rose wine

driest brut

nice to you

Crémant/vin mousseux, sparkling wine

Vin de maison, or house wine

regional vin de pays

a carafe or pitcher

...of water/wine/de vin

cheers! santé!

gueule de bois gueule de bois

Chapter 6

THE BEST HOTELS

First Arrondissement of Paris

Meurice Le

If you're considering staying in the heart of Paris, you might be wondering which accommodations are worthwhile to reserve and which you should avoid. The truth is that the Louvre Museum and other well-known attractions make the 1st arrondissement (district) of Paris one of the city's most visited tourist destinations. However, this does not imply that all of the local lodging is of a good standard. The best hotels in Paris's 1st arrondissement are listed here, with choices for almost any kind of traveller, whether you're going alone, with kids, or for a romantic trip.

Hôtel Mansart -

Esprit de France for Affordable Luxury and Classic Charm

Paris's Hotel Mansart, a room

Address: 5 Rue des Capucines, 75001 Paris, France Phone: +33 1 42 61 50 28 Courtesy of Hotel Mansart

This four-star hotel is situated behind the elegant Place Vendome and provides easy access to the Opera Garnier, the Palais Royal, and the Tuileries Gardens. Because of its upper-middle facilities, historical location, and boutique appeal, it is adored by tourists.

A listed structure from the 17th century that has been used as a hotel since the 19th century is where you'll find the Hôtel Mansart. Inside, tastefully decorated rooms and suites are created using traditional French design principles. Even the most basic accommodations include amenities like bathrobes and slippers, and the top-floor rooms and suites have plenty of natural light and little balconies with views of the famous Parisian rooftops. Some packages come with a cooked, organic breakfast that has received outstanding reviews from visitors.

Paris' Hotel du Continent

Designer furnishings and opulent extras: Inn on the Continental
Paris' Hotel du Continent
Address: 30 Rue du Mont Thabor, 75001 Paris, France Phone: +33 1 42 60 75 32 Courtesy of Hotel du Continent, Paris
This three-star boutique hotel has won praise for its fantasy-inspired interior design by French designer Christian Lacroix, plush accommodations, and consistently top-rated services. The hotel is a popular option with travelers seeking a central position and outstanding overall value because it is conveniently located near the Place de la Concorde, Place Vendome, and the Tuileries Gardens.
The five continents are represented by the hotel's 25 rooms. They have free Wi-Fi, air conditioning, a minibar, a safe, a satellite TV with foreign channels, bathrobes and slippers, and high-end toiletries. A concierge and

turn-down service are also available. Although some booking websites offer packages that include breakfast, the continental breakfast is typically an extra cost.

Hotel Le Meurice/Dorchester

Le Meurice, a romantic or special-occasion hotel in Paris
Hotel Le Meurice/Dorchester Collection is credited with this.
A stay at this five-star palace hotel can be perfect for a getaway with your significant other or a memorable family event. The recently renovated, lavishly furnished rooms and suites are indicative of an old-world Paris at its pinnacle. Le Meurice is certainly not subtle; it was designed to resemble the Palace of Versailles and its opulent royal furnishings.
The hotel has recently renovated rooms as well as a three-star Michelin restaurant run by renowned chef Alain Ducasse, a pastry shop with eye-catching creations from rising star Cedric Grolet, a full spa with soothing

treatments, and an afternoon tea that is simply blissful on a gloomy, chilly winter day.

The main drawback, please? This hotel is out of reach for the majority of tourists and their spending plans.

Paris's Hotel Louvre Opera

Hotel Paris Louvre Opéra is a good option for families and travelers on a budget.

Paris's Hotel Louvre Opera, room

Address: 4 Rue des Moulins, 75001 Paris, France Phone: +33 1 40 20 01 10 Courtesy of the Hotel Louvre Opera

Travelers seeking affordable pricing, reliable mid-range comforts, and family-friendly rules frequently choose this three-star hotel. The Best Western boutique hotel selection strikes a solid compromise between the trustworthy service you'd expect from a well-known chain and the unique design and atmosphere of a smaller hotel. The hotel honors Henri de Toulouse-Lautrec's paintings and the "Belle Epoque" period of late 19th-century Paris.

The standard rooms located inside the 17th-century structure are warm and invitingly furnished. They feature air conditioning, free Wi-Fi, welcome trays with bottled mineral water and flatscreen TVs with foreign channels. Small dogs and children are both welcome. A continental breakfast is frequently provided, and scheduling stays longer than two days typically results in lower rates.

Saint James Albany Paris Hotel and Spa

A tranquil spa retreat: At the Saint James Albany Paris Hotel and Spa, a superior room is available.

Saint James Albany Paris Hotel, with permission

Phone: +33 1 44 58 43 21 Address: 202 Rue de Rivoli, 75001 Paris, France

Travelers give this hotel on the upscale Rue de Rivoli across from the Tuileries great marks for its gorgeous rooms, fantastic location, and opulent services. This is one of the few four-star hotels in the heart of Paris that offers access to its spa and swimming pool.

The hotel's standard rooms come equipped with a minibar, safe, courtesy tray with coffee, tea, and mineral water, bathrobes and slippers, and L'Occitane en Provence products.
Visitors can unwind in the Turkish-style steam room and swim in the heated indoor pool at the on-site spa. The "Deep Nature" spa also provides a range of services, including everything from facials to full-body massages.

The hotel offers its customers a cash discount on meals at its partner restaurant, 202 Rivoli, which serves breakfast, brunch, lunch, and dinner.

DISNEYLAND HOTELS AND LODGE

You're going to be at Disneyland Paris, but you have no idea where to stay. We have compiled a list of every hotel around the park for you, including:

1. THE SANTA FE INN

Do you need a hotel close to Disneyland Paris that provides a genuine change of scenery? Discover the Santa Fe Hotel, the park's most economical establishment. You will be completely engulfed in the unique ambiance of the American Southwest and its famed route 66.

Are you prepared to experience the Route 66 vibe?

Antoine Predock, a native of New Mexico, created the Hotel Santa Fe. This hotel has Mexican characteristics throughout, giving it the charm of a motel. Take in the ambiance as soon as you pull into the parking area, which is reminiscent of a drive-in theater with a big screen showing the cartoon movie Cars. Beyond the architecture of the buildings, various decorations—such as a huge cactus like those in Arizona—add the ideal finishing touches to the outside atmosphere.

Disneyland Paris is a 20-minute stroll from the Hotel Santa Fe.

Spend a night or more at the Hotel Santa Fe.

There are a thousand rooms in this two-star hotel, spread out across forty structures on the property. The hotel is being refurbished in a manner reminiscent of Pixar's Cars animated film series. Numerous amenities are available to you at the Santa Fe hotel, including free wi-fi, a safe, and a complimentary shuttle to Disneyland Paris.

La Cantina, the hotel's buffet restaurant, is another option for dining. The Rio Grande Bar, an on-site bar with a Mexican theme, is also available.

2. DAVY CROCKETT RANCH BY DISNEY

At Disney Davy Crockett Ranch, a self-catering home away from home in a stunning natural location, settle in for a pleasant stay.

At Disney Davy Crockett Ranch®, fight for the independence of the frontier. You'll stay in your own cabin in the woods like a pioneer in the American colonial era, just a short drive from the Disney® Parks, on this nature retreat with lots of Disney enchantment.

Along with comfortable lodging, there is a tropical-themed pool with cascades and a jacuzzi, as well as a variety of family-friendly activities including ping-pong, basketball, and tennis. It has a space for a children's playground.

Superior Cabins

Superior Plus Near the village and amenities of Disney's Davy Crockett Ranch is a two-bedroom cabin. You'll have access to two showers, a hairdryer, cleaning supplies, and free cable internet. Additionally, your own outdoor deck with a BBQ and picnic table is a pleasant place

to relax. 4 single beds and 1 double bed. Family room.Determine Availability
Facilities
At Disney Davy Crockett Ranch, every cabin has:

A place to park
Disney and foreign TV networks
utensils, a microwave, a stove, a kettle and a refrigerator are all in the kitchen.
coffee maker
Larger bath towels are offered at the pool for a fee.

Guests with disabilities benefit from additional comfort and services in accessible cabins. To make a reservation, call the Disney Experts free at 0800 169 0737.

Disney's entertainment extras Ranch Davy Crockett
Extra Magic Time for visitors to Disney hotels. Enjoy one hour of Extra Magic Time at each of the Disney Parks prior to their scheduled opening.
Children's playground outside.

Indoor pool featuring slides, a waterfall, a river stream, and a whirlpool (open from 9:00 until 21:30).

Additional family sports, a covered tennis court, basketball, a fitness trail, etc.
Tree-top course featuring rope ladders, swings, and trapezes called Davy Crockett's Adventure. Suitable for individuals 1.10m and taller (extra cost).
Lucky Racoon Game Arcade is Fun for Kids (Fee).
A playground outside.
Indian-style camp with teepees and live entertainment on some days is called Campfire Circle.

Prices per adult start at
£145.00 GBP
for a stay of 1 night and 2 days, as well as passes to both Disney Parks!

Paris Marne-la-Vallée France Disneyland Resort at Disney's Davy Crockett Ranch

3. DISNEY NEWPORT BAY CLUB

The Disney Newport Bay Club is a celebration of all things maritime. Set your sights on leisure and take in the ambience of a 1920s New England home on Lake Disney's shoreline.
Travel back in time to the lakeside vacation cottages of the 1870s and experience what life was like at a yacht club. The Cape Cod-style Disney Newport Bay Club is a home brimming with nautical flair that is situated by the serene waters of Lake Disney.

There are numerous opportunities indoors to unwind in the warm environment of a New England sailing club. There are several dining options, the Captain's Quarters bar, a pool, sauna, whirlpool and a fitness center. Even body-sculpting massage is offered (for an additional fee).

The Captain's Quarters Bar offers a relaxing atmosphere with a nautical theme.

The Captain's Quarters Bar is a relaxing space with nautical decor.

Rooms

The nautical theme is carried throughout all of our bedrooms and suites by the tasteful white and navy blue decor.

Ask for rooms and suites.

Suites for a honeymoon, a president, and a resort come with breakfast in bed. With a living space and stunning lake views, unwind in elegance. 2 beds: 1 double and 1 couch bed.Determine Availability

Facilities

At Disney Newport Bay Club, every one of our rooms has:

Conditional air

Internet access via WiFi for free

Disney and foreign TV networks

secure hair dryer

Hotel rooms that can be accessed by people with impairments offer more comfort and services. To make a reservation, call our Disney Experts free at 0800 169 0737.

In the nautically inspired rooms and suites, experience the yacht club way of life.
In the nautically inspired rooms and suites, experience the yacht club way of life.
How far are the Disney Parks away?
The Disney Parks are accessible through a short, free shuttle bus ride or a 15-minute stroll through Disney Village from Disney Newport Bay Club.

Taverns and restaurants
Drink and eat at:

Enjoy one or two aperitifs at the Captain's Quarters, a bar with a nautical motif.
At the Cape Cod Buffet Restaurant, international flavors converge in a seaside environment.
Yacht Club is a welcoming eatery that offers a variety of international specialties.
Experience international specialties in the restaurant of the Yacht Club.
In the restaurant at the Yacht Club, savor worldwide specialties.
Extracurricular Activities at Disney Newport Bay Club®

free parking for cars.

Extra Magic Time for visitors to Disney hotels. Enjoy one hour of Extra Magic Time at each of the Disney Parks prior to their scheduled opening.

Disney Hotel Newport Bay Club's fitness center Visit the hotel's gym, which is equipped with a variety of fitness tools, to stay in shape.

There are two swimming pools where you can swim in the indoor and outdoor pools and unwind in the sauna (the indoor pool is accessible from 7:00 until 21:45; the outdoor section's hours vary with the season).

If you're looking for Disney presents and seasonal necessities, Bay Boutique is the place to start.

In select areas of the hotel, wi-fi and internet connection are accessible for a fee.

Kids can play in a designated area near the bar while their parents watch them.

With a variety of coin-operated game machines, the Sea Horse Club Game Arcade.

a special children's buffet.

4. SEQUOIA INN

SEQUOIA LODGE

Reconnect with nature in a woodland lodge that has all the modern conveniences.
At Disney Sequoia Lodge, you'll feel right at home if you enjoy being outside. It's a cozy getaway at the edge of Lake Disney, surrounded by dense pines, and is only a 15 minutes' stroll via Disney Village from the Disney Parks.

Walking by the lake, a leisurely swim or workout, dinner and drinks, or, for younger explorers, a mini-adventure in the pool or play area, are just a few of the options to unwind here.

In the Redwood Bar and Lounge, unwind with a drink while sitting by the fire.
In the Redwood Bar and Lounge, unwind with a drink while sitting by the fire.
Rooms: Cozy lodge-style rooms with hardwood furnishings and classic accents that honor

19th-century American crafts will make you feel at home.

Check Availability
Facilities
At Disney Sequoia Lodge, each of our rooms includes:

Conditional air
Disney and foreign TV networks
Hairdryer
Hotel rooms that can be accessed by people with impairments offer more comfort and services. To make a reservation, call our Disney Experts free at 0800 169 0737*.

Warm lodge-style lodging with wooden furnishings and conventional accents
Warm lodge-style accommodations with wooden furnishings and antique accents.
How far are the Disney Parks away?
The Disney Parks are only a short, free shuttle-bus ride away from Disney Sequoia Lodge after a 15-minute walk through Disney Village.

Taverns and restaurants
Drink and eat at:

- Hunter's Grill offers a delectable buffet with flavors from around the world.

- Beaver Creek Tavern is a tavern-style eatery serving traditional meals from North America.

- Redwood Bar and Lounge - unwind with a drink and a snack while sitting by the fire.

The Hunter's Grill offers a delicious buffet with delicacies from around the world.
The Hunter's Grill offers a tantalizing buffet with delicacies from around the world.

Extras for entertainment at Disney Sequoia Lodge
free parking for cars.
Extra Magic Time for visitors to Disney hotels. Enjoy one hour of Extra Magic Time at each of the Disney Parks prior to their scheduled opening.

Both indoor and outdoor pools are open (the indoor pool is open from 7:00 am to 21:45 pm, while the outdoor area is open at a time determined by the season).
fitness center.

Fun for Children
- Water features include a waterfall and a slide in the pool.

- places to play outside.

- kid-friendly menus.

Prices per adult start at
£163.00GBP
for a stay of 1 night and 2 days, as well as passes to both Disney Parks!
Sequoia Lodge by Disney
Address: B.P. 114, 77777 Marne-la-Vallée, France Disneyland Resort Paris

5. CHEYENNE INN

HOTEL DISNEY CHEYENNE

Hotel Disney Cheyenne
At the Disney Hotel Cheyenne, experience a bit of the Old West. With old-style saloons, waggons, and rootin' tootin' cowboy friendliness everywhere, you'll think you've walked onto the set of a Western.
Hang up your ten-gallon hat in one of the snug, friendly rooms at the Disney Hotel Cheyenne and take a trip back to the American Old West.

An entire frontier-style settlement with a saloon, store, café, and outdoor spaces filled with cowpoke charm is available for exploration. Come on down where you'll find welcoming cowboys sporting their rodeo regalia, yee ha!

Throughout the hotel, you'll find Old West-inspired charm.
Throughout the hotel, you'll find Old West-inspired charm.

Every room is furnished in a wild west theme, from the bucking bronco tiles in the bathroom to the saddles and stars on the bedheads.

Check Facilities Availability
At the Disney Hotel Cheyenne, each of our rooms includes:

An overhead fan
Disney and foreign TV networks
Safe
Hotel rooms that can be accessed by people with impairments offer more comfort and services. To make a reservation, call our Disney Experts free at 0800 169 0737.

In your Toy Story-themed quarters, hang up your spurs for the evening.
In your Toy Story-themed quarters, hang up your spurs for the evening.
How far are the Disney Parks away?
The Disney Hotel Cheyenne is a short, free shuttle-bus ride from Disney Village or a 15-minute walk from the Disney Parks.

Taverns and restaurants

Drink and eat at:

Red Garter Saloon offers a variety of cocktails along with country and western music.
All-you-can-eat dinner buffets are available at Chuckwagon Café for your entire herd.
Dinner buffet available at Chuckwagon all day long.
Dinner buffet at Chuck Waggon that is all-you-can-eat.

Extras for entertainment at the Disney Hotel Cheyenne
Extra Magic Time for visitors to Disney hotels. Enjoy one hour of Extra Magic Time at each of the Disney Parks prior to their scheduled opening.
free parking for cars.

For all your Disney Character presents and mementos, as well as seasonal items, visit the general store.
Fun for Children
At the Little Sheriffs children's corner, kids can play while their parents watch them.

In addition, area with TV and games.
A teepee-filled outdoor play area called Fort Apache.

Nevada Game Arcade offers a variety of coin-operated gaming devices.
Children can ride ponies on the trail (for an additional fee and depending on the season).
Prices per adult start at

£163.00 GBP
for a stay of 1 night and 2 days, as well as passes to both Disney Parks!
B.P. 115 77777 Disney Hotel Cheyenne Disneyland Resort France's Marne-la-Vallée

6. NEW YORK'S DISNEY HOTEL - THE ART OF MARVEL

At Disney's Hotel New York - The Art of Marvel, achieve heroic heights.
The Disney Hotel New York - The Art of Marvel, located just a Thor hammer's throw from the

Disney Parks, combines all the flair and refinement of contemporary Manhattan with over 350 pieces of original MARVEL artwork.

Fly over to Super Hero Station, the only location in any of our Disney Hotels where you may meet Marvel Super Heroes, to pick up some heroic mementos, explore your inner artist, and pick up some heroic keepsakes.

Utilize the hotel's cutting-edge amenities as well. Swim in the Metro Pool, unwind in the sauna and steam room, or get together for a fun workout in the indoor Metro Health Club and outdoor Hero Training Zone.

Admire the unique, original artwork displayed throughout the property.
Admire the unique, original artwork found throughout the property.
The rooms are slick and fashionable, with the atmosphere of a modern city setting, and they are decorated with works by Marvel.

Ask for rooms and suites.

Superior Family Room - With space for up to 6 people, the entire family will have plenty of room in this room, which also features MARVEL artwork and designs inspired by Manhattan.SuperHeroes Suite - Each SuperHero Suite features selected, exclusive Marvel art, as well as other perks to make your stay even more enjoyable.Spider-Man room - Each room is uniquely designed and features décor that is inspired by Spider-Man. Enjoy additional advantages while you're there.

The Avengers Suite honors the enduring Super Heroes in a way never previously possible with artwork based on Captain America, Iron Man, and Thor. Take advantage of additional incentives as well while you are there.Reach new heights in the Presidential Suite, which is decorated with unique MARVEL portraits and is spread out across two storeys.

 Enjoy additional privileges and unwind in this Disney hotel's finest amenities.

Determine Availability
Facilities

At the Disney Hotel New York - The Art of Marvel, every room has:

Conditional air
Internet access via WiFi for free
Minibar
Disney and foreign TV networks
a securing deposit box
Hairdryer
Telephone
luggage assistance

Hotel rooms that can be accessed by people with impairments offer more comfort and services. To make a reservation, call our Disney Experts free at 0800 169 0737.

How far are the Disney Parks away?
The Disney Hotel New York - The Art of Marvel is a short, free shuttle-bus ride from the Disney Parks or a ten-minute walk through Disney Village.

Taverns and restaurants
Drink and eat at:

After a long day, unwind at Manhattan Restaurant, an Italian-style restaurant with homemade food and upscale decor.
Enjoy a taste of New York in the art deco-inspired buffet restaurant Downtown, which offers a variety of cuisines to suit all palates.

Skyline Bar is a great place to take in the Manhattan skyline while sipping on a beverage. Keep a lookout for any friendly faces flying by while you enjoy the view.
At Skyline Bar, sip on a classic cocktail while admiring the skyline.

At Skyline Bar, sip a traditional cocktail while admiring the panoramic views.

Extras in Entertainment at the Disney Hotel in New York - Extra Magic Time with The Art of Marvel for visitors to Disney hotels.

The Art of Marvel Extra Magic Time for Disney hotel guests is one of the entertainment extras at the Disney Hotel New York. Enjoy one hour of Extra Magic Time at each of the Disney Parks prior to their scheduled opening.

Shop in New York for all your Marvel memorabilia, including rare rarities.

The only location in any of our Disney Hotels where you may meet your beloved Super Heroes is Super Hero Station.

Marvel Design Studio is a place where you and your kids may explore your creative side and discover how to create your own comic book.

The Fitness Centre is open every day of the week for anyone looking to pack on the pounds like the Hulk.

In the sauna, steam room, and indoor and outdoor pools, unwind and rejuvenate.

Prices per adult start at

£197.00 GBP

for a stay of 1 night and 2 days, as well as passes to both Disney Parks!

The Disneyland Resort Paris Avenue Goscinny Marne-la-Vallée France is home to the Disney Hotel New York - The Art of Marvel.

7. HOTEL DISNEYLAND

Welcome to the Disneyland Hotel, the pinnacle five-star royal residence where everyone's fantasy of leading a life fit for a king or queen is realized.
Learn about the ultimate five-star Disney hotel where everyone can live like a king or queen, enjoy fairy tales, and create their own.

You once upon a time starts at Disneyland Hotel, which has its own entrance to Disneyland® Park. It continues during your stay as you dine, drink, sleep, and socialize in opulent settings. Hold court alongside the regal Disney characters as well.

A stunning change is now taking place at the Disneyland Hotel. On January 25, 2024, the royal reopening will take place; reserve your room today!

Discover tastefully furnished rooms and suites with opulent facilities and services.

Ask for Suites
Soon to be! A private elevator to Disneyland Park, extra amenities, and access to the Castle Club Lounge for breakfast with Disney Princess characters, tea time, and all-day soft drinks are all included in our collection of enchanting suites.

Enjoy regal luxury in the Rapunzel-themed Rapunzel Signature Suite, where a mystical golden blossom shines and lanterns float by the window. The Sleeping Beauty Signature Suite is a stately suite that has been charmed with mythical luxuries by the spell of the Sleeping Beauty. one king-size bed and one couch bed.
Determine Availability
Facilities
At the Hotel at Disneyland, each of our rooms has:

Conditional air
Internet access via WiFi for free
Minibar

Disney and foreign TV networks
theme-related bathroom supplies
Safe
espresso coffee maker and tea maker
Hairdryer
Hotel rooms that can be accessed by people with impairments offer more comfort and services. To make a reservation, call our Disney Experts free at 0800 169 0737.

How far are the Disney Parks away?
The Walt Disney Studios Park is three minutes' walk from the Disneyland Hotel, which is located immediately by the entrance to Disneyland Park.

Taverns and restaurants
Come as our guest and savour the finest meals at:

The best eating experience at Disneyland Paris is La Table de Lumière. Together with the Disney Princesses and their princes, savour the finest French cuisine.
Enjoy a sumptuous feast at the Royal Banquet while taking in decor honouring the heritage of

royal Disney families. Enjoy a meal with Disney characters as they are dressed to the nines.

Enjoy delectable teatime snacks, special champagne from the Disneyland Hotel or traditional, modern and even family-friendly cocktails at Fleur de Lys Bar.

Reservations at restaurants

Because of the popularity of our restaurants, making reservations in advance is strongly advised to avoid disappointment. Make sure to reserve your table well in advance for table service restaurants and buffet restaurants (up to 12 months in advance for Disney Hotel Guests) for peace of mind and more options. The simplest and fastest way to book is using the official Disneyland Paris app.

You can also verify the availability of dining reservations by phoning the Disney Dining Reservation Service at any time prior to arrival at 0800 085 0671. Please be aware that you must reference the Disneyland Paris reference number that is printed on your travel documents.

Additionally, you can schedule a meal with the hotel's concierge.

You have the unique chance to schedule dinner at your hotel before arrival as a Guest staying at the Disneyland Hotel!

Amusement and extras
The Disneyland Hotel's extras
free parking for cars.
Extra Magic Time for visitors to Disney hotels. Enjoy one hour of Extra Magic Time at each of the Disney Parks prior to their scheduled opening.
With a pool, sauna, and five-star exercise centre, The Crystal Pool & Health Club.
Offering spa services such as massages, manicures, and pedicures, as well as treatments specifically for children (for an additional fee), the Disneyland Hotel Spa by Clarins.
Discover unique products from the Disneyland Hotel at the Royal Collection Boutique.
Fun for Children
Young princes and princesses between the ages of 4 and 11 can partake in enchanting activities,

interactive storytelling, and artistic workshops at the Royal Kids Club.

Hold court with Disney Characters in a royal one-on-one encounter with Disney Royal Encounter. Remember to reserve yours on the Disneyland Paris app up to seven days in advance of your visit.

Little princesses and princes can live out their fairytale fantasies with the help of My Royal Dream, a royal makeover. Additional charges apply. Order yours in advance using the Disneyland Paris app, or when you get there,
at the Royal Collection Boutique
or Concierge Desk.
£267.00 GBP
for a stay of 1 night and 2 days, as well as passes to both Disney Parks!

77777 Marne-la-Vallée,
France Disneyland Hotel
Disneyland Resort Paris B.P. 100

8. LES VILLAGES NATURE PARIS

The Aqualagon at Les Villages Nature Paris

Les Villages Nature Paris, which is not far from Disneyland Paris, offers a different kind of wonder.
This is a genuinely unique holiday experience that will make you feel at one with nature, whether you're with family or friends. Explore five distinct worlds and the unforgettable experiences they provide, then unwind in a rural retreat or a wellness oasis that serves as your home away from home.

Determine AvailabilityHaving fun as a family at Les Villages Nature de Paris
Everyone Can Have Fun
Les Villages Nature Paris offers a wide range of activities, so there is something for every age group. Additionally, a variety of sports and entertainment are included in your stay.

However, some of these activities may have additional costs and may need to be reserved in advance.

Les Villages Nature Paris Experience's immersive worlds Five Virtual Worlds
The waterpark and heated open-air lagoon at Aqualagon provide excitement and relaxation. Visit BelleVie Farm to interact with animals, stroll through the Extraordinary Gardens, learn about the Forest of Legends, and luxuriate at the Lakeside Promenade.

At Les Villages Nature Paris, travelers can stay in luxurious accommodations.
Elegant Accommodations
Choose accommodations with the atmosphere you desire for a memorable trip. There is something for everyone, from quaint rural getaways to wellness havens.
Les Villages Nature Paris Accessibility
Les Villages Nature Paris is difficult for visitors coming by Eurostar or by plane to get due to its location. It's ideal for those who want to drive themselves via P&O Ferries or Le Shuttle (formerly known as Eurotunnel), though.

Speak to our Disney Experts freephone at 0800 169 0733 for suggestions on how to organize your trip.

Prices per adult start at

£180.00 GBP
for a stay of 1 night and 2 days, as well as passes to both Disney Parks!

Apartments at Les Villages Nature Paris Immersive Worlds
Les Villages Nature Paris offers a Woodland Retreat.
A vacation to remember spent at one with nature and filled with extraordinary experiences:
a full-service resort featuring luxurious, environmentally friendly self-catering lodging. A unique swimming paradise with heated open-air lagoons and waterslides. Ideal location for visiting the Disney Parks and close to Disneyland Paris. Activities, shows, and workshops for families are included throughout your stay. Delicious food is served all day long,

featuring meals cooked using seasonal ingredients that are acquired locally.

Chapter 7

101 DISNEYLAND PARIS TIPS: Tips And Tricks

Many people's first experience with an international park is a trip to Disneyland Paris. Others' first experience with a Disney park. There are numerous things that can either make your holiday more enjoyable or save you time and money. Based on experiences visiting Disneyland Paris, here are 101 pieces of advice.

Knowing what not to do at Disneyland Paris is almost as crucial as knowing what to do.

Making sure that everyone has a pleasant time is my aim with these Disneyland Paris travel suggestions. You expect to find a convenient spot to dine when you feel hungry at seven o'clock? You'll have bad times. Do you anticipate friendly interactions with cast members who wish you a "magical day"? You'll have bad times. You anticipate a work of art with a similar topic when you visit Walt Disney Studios Park after seeing Parc Disneyland. You'll have bad times.

This list might continue forever. Although it could appear that this is being said in jest, it is not. I believe that one of the main reasons Disneyland Paris divides people is because many visitors arrive with expectations formed by their visits to Walt Disney World, whereas Disneyland Paris is very different from that. My assessment is that it's different, but not in a negative sense; rather, it's different in a way that calls for modifying expectations.

Let's get started with the 101 finest Disneyland Paris suggestions now.

- Compare prices when purchasing a holiday package on the Disneyland Paris websites in the US, UK, Germany, and other European countries.

- You might receive a better value by making your reservation through a different version of the website because Disney (controversially) offers different pricing and promotions to different areas.

- Even though every counter service restaurant has a set menu that includes an entree, a side or sides, and a drink, you can save money by only ordering the meal. A la carte entrees are offered at almost all restaurants (and are more usually mentioned on the printed menus given to guests), despite only being listed on a few menu boards.

- Ponchos (rain is a typical occurrence in France) and external battery chargers for your phone are two essential items to bring. These are only two of the unusual items on our post about the Unusual Disney Packing List.

- Sequoia Lodge is our preferred on-site lodging option for Disneyland Paris. Consider it to be the Wilderness Lodge of Paris. In this piece about the Disneyland Paris hotels, we discuss the additional accommodations.

- If you decide to eat at more expensive establishments (such Auberge de Cendrillon, Bistrot Chez Remy, and California Grill), the Half and Full Board Meal Packages may result in cost savings for your Disneyland Paris eating experience. Here is a detailed list of what is included in each package.

- Restaurants cannot reorder sugary beverages because of a recent French rule. Few restaurants at Disneyland Paris offered refills even before this regulation, but as a result of it, even the Coke Freestyle machines that are being added at places like Five Guys will only fill one cup.

- The experience is enhanced by staying on-site at a Disneyland Paris hotel, although the prices are absurdly high for the level of service. We advise lodging off-site at Val d'Europe, which is close by and is the RER train stop before Disneyland Paris.

- Our favorite recommendation for off-site lodging in Val d'Europe is the low-cost, apartment-style Hipark Serris, which is just a 15-minute stroll from the parks.

- There are lengthy supper lineups at popular restaurants at Disneyland Paris because many of the eateries close at or near 5 o'clock. 30-45 minute wait times are not unusual just to place an order. If you are not a senior citizen, we advise delaying dinner until Disney Village shuts (Earl of Sandwich, Five Guys, and even McDonald's are acceptable choices).

- In view of the aforementioned law, I advise bringing your own "fix" if you're a coffee junkie like us. Both the Starbucks and Trader Joe's packets I've used in the past have been good to me.

- Consider splitting your stay between a hotel close to Disneyland Paris and a hotel in the heart of Paris for that section of your trip. The RER line will take approximately an hour to travel from the city center to Disneyland Paris (and vice versa); it is not feasible to commute back and forth.

- Purchase an annual pass for Disneyland Paris. It makes financial sense if you're staying for four days. Due to the benefits and reductions, it may make sense even for a 3-day vacation.

- Walt Disney Studios Park is awful; there is no other way to phrase it. Despite the park's few compelling features, we rarely stay longer than a half-day.

- Not before your vacation, but while you are there, buy your youngster a character dress. I realize that goes against what we've said in past postings, but that holds true for American theme parks where princess dresses are expensive but poorly made. The ones in Disneyland Paris are equally pricey and lovely. One of these outfits would be perfect for purchase.

- No matter where you stay in France, a voltage converter must be packed. I advise using something straightforward and affordable, like this grounded 2 in 1 plug adapter. If you're like me and charge the majority of your devices through USB these days, think about connecting it with this small 6-port USB charging station.

- For morning Extra Magic Hours, the majority of attractions are closed, and those that are open may have long lines by the second hour of EMH. I advise beginning with Peter Pan's Flight and repeating it twice.

- Before your journey, download the official Disneyland Paris app. It's helpful for wait times as well as restaurant hours, which can occasionally be erratic.

- My favorite time of year to visit Disneyland Paris is around Christmas. Beautiful decorations and a wonderful holiday atmosphere may be found here.

- Access to Extra Magic Hours is one of the valuable benefits of Disneyland Paris Annual Passes, which is crucial if you're staying off-site. Additionally, the Infinity Annual Pass offers VIP reserved seats for the parade and Disney Illuminations, which can save you a tonne of time.

- Take patience with you. Due to a variety of variables, including the fact that Disneyland Paris is a melting pot of various European cultures, "guests behaving badly" seems to be a bigger problem there than in the American parks.

- In Europe, smoking is also considerably more prevalent, and you'll frequently see smokers outside designated smoking places.

- Speaking of France, Disneyland Paris is there. Obviously. It is therefore a development of French and European culture rather than American culture. If you're an American, go there expecting a different culture. Although it should be evident to everyone, Disneyland Paris' underlying culture is the source of the majority of criticisms.

- Numerous drinking fountains can be found around the parks, and many establishments will provide you free tap water (with request); we advise taking a bottle to fill up. (Excellent for making your own coffee.)

- Take the TGV train from Charles de Gaulle airport rather than the RER or shuttles. The RER will require you to travel to downtown Paris and change trains, making the trip take more than an hour. The TGV is a 10-minute ride. TGV is less frequent and more expensive, but it is more convenient.

- At Disneyland Paris, it has been known to snow and turn chilly. Be sure to read our post on what to pack for winter at Disney if you're traveling between October and March.

- We strongly advise staking yourself a location on the backside of a flower planter in the Central Plaza (hub) for a guaranteed clear view of Disney Illuminations, the nightly spectacle. As Shoulder kids' are very common in Disneyland Paris, this will make sure that no one is standing in front of you, which is vital. There's nothing worse than having a vista that was otherwise stunning and spoiled suddenly!

- At Disneyland Paris, weekends are the busiest days of the week because local Parisians also frequent the parks on their off days in addition to out-of-town visitors.

- Pin trading is still practiced at Disneyland Paris, albeit less frequently (at least, that's my view).

- There are numerous incredible themed eateries at Disneyland Paris. In fact, we advise basing part of your dining decisions on the concept of the restaurant.

- For owners of annual passes, luggage storage outside of the parks is free. On arrival and departure days (or if you brought a tripod and don't want to carry it around all day), this is a very useful convenience.

- Phantom Manor, which is a combination of the odd and brilliant, is Disneyland Paris' take on Haunted Mansion.

- The two off-site hotels I suggest are Relais Spa and Hotel L'Elysée Val d'Europe if you'd rather take the RER train to Disneyland Paris than walk there. Having said that, Val d'Europe is a brand-new development, so it's unlikely that you'll find an unclean or out-of-date hotel there. Another option is to use Airbnb, which frequently has a number of houses in this region.

- Make sure to stop by Guest Services at your resort hotel or in the parks to pick up a button commemorating the occasion if you're celebrating one.

- The Sleeping Beauty Castle, also known as Le Château de la Belle au Bois Dormant, is the most exquisite Disney castle ever built. To learn how to photograph the Sleeping Beauty Castle in Paris, read our essay on photography tips.

- Between 2021 and 2024, Walt Disney Studios Park is undergoing a significant expansion. Three additional lands will be added, and the park will be redesigned.

The Avengers Campus will make its debut first, then the Frozen Land, then a Star Wars: Galaxy's Edge replica.

- My first suggestion is to bring protein bars or buy groceries and create something yourself if you're eating breakfast without vouchers.

- If you don't think that sounds appetizing, pick up a snack at McDonald's or Starbucks in Disney Village before entering the park. .

- Since the cuisine at in-park eateries like Cafe Hyperion and Cable Car Bake Shop isn't particularly good and they might get very busy with people redeeming vouchers, it's preferable to spend your valuable early morning time on attractions instead!

- Disneyland Paris can get crowded during the summer and during school breaks. No matter when you go, it is advised to use our 1-Day Disneyland Paris Itinerary as a guide for a successful plan.

- Despite the fact that we don't have a 1-Day Itinerary for Walt Disney Studios Park, I suggest rope dropping Crush's Coaster before riding Ratatouille.

- The Adventure solo. I rarely spend more than two to three hours in the Walt Disney Studios Park during a visit (I typically stay three days at Disneyland Paris).

- There is an Auchan Supermarket Val d'Europe nearby that has all the food you may possibly need. This can be a wise, cost-effective location because many of the hotels in Val d'Europe have kitchens and because the food at Disneyland Paris is of high quality.

- The Disney Gallery in Disney Village provides a wide selection of exquisite artwork, including custom-made attraction posters.

- In addition to a matted print of the Phantom Manor poster, I have purchased a collection of 12 posters (similar to the calendar marketed in the U.S., but without the calendar element).

- Every day of your trip, be sure to show respect to the dragon that slumbers beneath the castle.

- Recently, Disney's Newport Bay Club Hotel completed a top-to-bottom renovation that earned it an extra star in its ranking.

- The hotel has significantly improved, and right now it would be our top choice for an on-site hotel. (I adore Sequoia Lodge, but the renovated accommodations at Newport are nicer.)

- Mickey Mouse makes an appearance at the Main Street U.S.A. Train Station during Mickey's Kiss Goodnight to wave goodbye to guests and recite a few lines.

- This starts roughly 10 minutes after Disney Illuminations ends and continues sporadically throughout the next 10-15 minutes.

- Compare costs from both the Marne-la-Vallee station (in Disneyland Paris) and Gare du Nord (downtown Paris) if taking the Eurostar to or from Disneyland Paris. I discovered that rates were better outside of Gare du Nord when I traveled from Paris to London.

- Dress formally. This doesn't really apply to Disneyland Paris as much as it does to the rest of Paris, but it's important to remember because you'll probably be going to both.

- I advise you to stay away from athletic wear and revealing apparel, both of which are uncommon in France. There are two compelling reasons to dress decently, even if you "don't care" about your appearance: you'll get better service and you won't be a target for pickpockets.

- A lot of the Fantasyland attractions close early because of the midnight spectacle. In particular for Peter Pan's Flight, we advise doing this early in the morning, ideally during Extra Magic Hours.

- Head to the rockwork at Discoveryland's entrance and select a spot along the handrail with a clear view of Le Château de la Belle au Bois Dormant for a nice "secret" viewing location for Disney Illuminations.

- The uncommon characters in Disneyland Paris are well-known, and meet & greets are hugely popular overall in theme parks. Making characters your first stop during Extra Magic Hours is a smart move if characters are important to you.

- The Disneyland Paris hotels' bars and lounges are frequently open late and several provide excellent ambiance for a nightcap after the park shuts. For detailed advice, go to our Guide to Drinking in Disneyland Paris.

- Many parts on the Big Thunder Mountain Railroad fail. It did not open with the park in many spots on our most recent trip, which caused traffic jams and confusion due to rope drop crowds. Due to the probable bottleneck, we advise rope dropping Big Thunder and doing so via Adventureland.

- The best counter service burger at Disneyland Paris can be found at Five Guys, which is situated on the "back" side of Disney Village.

- It's okay to order a distinctly American dinner in France because the counter service food in the parks is generally subpar.

- I participated in the Disneyland Paris 5K and Half Marathon, and I thought it was the best runDisney event available. It also falls on Halloween, which is a fantastic time to visit Disneyland Paris!

- In comparison to their U.S. outlets, Earl of Sandwich at Disney Village offers a lot more selections (including BBQ ribs!) and is a fantastic deal for dining out.

- Additionally, there is free WiFi available here.

- Fantastic Italian ice cream can be found at Fantasia Gelati.

- I recommend ordering a cup with three scoops and two crepes for two people. Eat the third scoop alone after taking two of the scoops out of the cup and placing them on top of the crepes.

- The Fantasia flavor is wonderful (but not as good on a crepe!), tasting like a blend of birthday cake and cotton candy.

- The Star Wars event "Legends of the Force" will be celebrated at Walt Disney Studios Park.

- While some of the Season of the Force entertainment is now accessible year-round, others (such as the signature Star Wars.

- A Galactic festival evening spectacular) will only be accessible during the short-lived festival.

- Our recommendation for the top table service restaurant for Disney fans is Walt's - An American Restaurant.

- Since the menu was revised, the food has improved noticeably, and the interior decor, which is inspired by Walt Disney and the lands of Disneyland Paris, is amazing.

- Now, this environment surpasses Club 33.

- Hyperspace Mountain, Crush's Coaster, Ratatouille: L'Aventure Totalement Toquee de Remy, Toy Soldiers Parachute Drop, and RC Racer all have single riders accessible.

- I advise Cowboy Cookout BBQ if you are forced to eat dinner in Disneyland Paris. It is a counter service restaurant with far fewer lines (and better cuisine) than other places, and it is typically open later.

- For the ideal way to cap off the day, get in line for Big Thunder Mountain Railroad about five minutes before the park closes. You won't only get to enjoy the best attraction at Disneyland Paris with little to no wait, but you'll also get to do it as Disney Illuminations fireworks erupt over you.

- Make a reservation for the Sunday Brunch at Inventions at the Disneyland Hotel if you enjoy characters. The lunch features tasty cuisine, a lovely setting and perspective, and a cast of odd (and occasionally uncommon) characters.

- For the ideal way to cap off the day, get in line for Big Thunder Mountain Railroad about five minutes before the park closes.

- You won't only get to enjoy the best attraction at Disneyland Paris with little to no wait, but you'll also get to do it as Disney Illuminations fireworks erupt over you.

- Make a reservation for the Sunday Brunch at Inventions at the Disneyland Hotel if you enjoy characters. The lunch features tasty cuisine, a lovely setting and perspective, and a cast of odd (and occasionally uncommon) characters.

- The buffet at Agrabah Cafe Restaurant is first-rate and beautifully themed. It is the best dining choice at Disneyland Paris in terms of value.

- Both parks provide bilingual guided tours in French, English, and Spanish. These explore the parks' history, particulars, well-kept mysteries, architecture, etc.

- These trips are extra, and they don't come with preferential entry to the attractions.

- For information on tour availability and timings during your visit, go to City Hall in Disneyland Paris or Studio Services in Walt Disney Studios Park.

- Up to an hour after the park shuts, Main Street's stores are still open. Once you are unable to take rides, go shopping.

- Dole Whips, which are currently offered at Disneyland Paris, have a well-deserved reputation. Although i believe there has been a bit too much buzz surrounding this snack, everyone seems to enjoy them, thus...

- The Fantasyland Disneyland Railroad Station typically has the least waits; oddly, on even moderately crowded days, waiting for this attraction can be quite long.

- With good reason, the Disneyland Hotel will be totally shuttered for renovations for at least a year. It is currently planned to reopen in 2024 after undergoing a complete redesign.

- The "newest" and most modern hotel at Disneyland Paris is Disney's Hotel New York — The Art of Marvel.

- The Indiana Jones ride in Paris, Indiana Jones and the Temple of Peril, is nothing like the Indiana Jones attraction in Disneyland; it is a pretty forgettable, basic coaster.

- If you don't love yourself, stay away from Cafe Hyperion. Skip it, even if it's the only eatery open late. It is preferable to go hungry.

- The cat is Figaro. (Unfortunately, Disneyland Paris does not have a sign stating as such. Incredible "fail," Imagineers.

- Despite our harsh criticism of the Walt Disney Studios Park, Mickey and the Magician is one of the world's top Disney stage productions. You might even end up repeating this more than once, so save it for bad weather!

- The Explorer's Club was the previous name of Colonel Hathi's Pizza Outpost, and there are many interesting artifacts from that era scattered all over the dining area.

- The Central Plaza's curved sidewalk, which is located immediately outside of Frontierland, is the greatest place to watch Disney Stars on Parade. You will get a clear view of the floats approaching you while the castle is in the distance (ideal for photography!).

- The Hotel Santa Fe is home to a volcano. Although it's not nearly as cool as it may sound, it's the kind of thing that makes the trek from one of the local resorts worth it in order to see or take pictures of.

- The steak on the highest tier of the set menus at Bistro Chez Remy, which is by far the greatest restaurant in Walt Disney Studios Park, is excellent. (The less expensive steak, less so.)

- Inversions are a part of Hyperspace Mountain, which is much more intense in Paris.

- Several dining options at Disneyland Paris offer foie gras, a popular (and contentious) French delicacy.

- Bastille Day is celebrated on July 14 each year in France, and Disneyland Paris celebrates by putting on a magnificent fireworks display when the park closes.

Videos show that despite the large crowds, it is worthwhile.

- The view of Fantasyland and Sleeping Beauty Castle from the top of Queen of Hearts Castle alone makes Alice's Curious Labyrinth worthwhile, especially after sunset. You can directly access the castle viewpoint by entering the maze through the exit on days when it's not busy.

- A credit card with a chip is required for Disneyland Paris. In Europe, chip and pin credit cards are required, although chip and signature cards, which are the new requirement in the US, also function.

- Don't miss the Nautilus, the Swiss Family Treehouse, the Enchanted Aladdin Passage, the Château de la Belle au Bois Dormant Walk-through, or Adventure Isle. All of them are walkthroughs, but they are all quite good.

- Explore both Main Street Arcades; they serve a utilitarian purpose (protecting visitors from snow or rain), but also feature lovely embellishments that make them worthwhile explorations.

- While the cast members at Disneyland Paris are generally understanding of visitors who don't speak French, it's a good habit (all around France!) to start any French conversation by saying, "I don't speak French. Are you English-speaking? (I am not fluent in French. You speak English, right?

- For chilly nights, the Sequoia Lodge's fireplace in Redwood Bar & Lounge and the outdoor fire pit by the Red Garter Saloon at the Hotel Cheyenne are both ideal.

- A brand-new, environmentally friendly tourism project called Villages Nature is being jointly created by Disney and prominent Imagineers like Joe Rohde. We haven't stayed there yet, but it seems like a fascinating and distinctive place to stay while visiting Disneyland Paris.

- Of all the Disney parks, Disneyland Paris boasts the best, functional barbershop. An extravagant barbershop in Chicago served as the inspiration for the interior theme.

- The Paddywagon is one of many unusual cars that ply Main Street, but it's our choice as the coolest/most distinctive. On the right side of Town Square, look for its stop.

- Cowboy Cookout BBQ's potato wedges are the ideal afternoon treat. I strongly advise going at a quiet time, getting a side of these, and relaxing by the fire pit.

- Nowadays, character breakfast is served in the Plaza Gardens Restaurant; reservations are required.

- The Disney hotel's Club level offers access to a private lounge with drinks all day long as well as a buffet breakfast.

- When watching parades or Disney Illuminations, avoid standing on the grass. No matter what other visitors are doing, simply don't.

- The "inhabitants" of Disneyland Paris have a variety of sound effects and dialogues throughout the park. On Main Street, you can hear several of these things, like a dentist drilling and piano lessons. Crowd noises during the day can mask them, but at night they can be clearly heard.

- Both Walt Disney Studios Park and Disneyland Paris do not sell chewing gum.

- The only castle park that offers beer and wine at counter service restaurants is Disneyland Paris. This modification was made soon after the park's debut to put it in line with French cultural expectations. Disneyland Paris does not have a problem with public intoxication.

- There are several Easter Eggs and references to the Imagineers who worked on the project at Boot Hill Cemetery outside Phantom Manor.

- Ask about the character meet & greet schedule in your hotel if you're a guest at a Disney hotel. In contrast to the meet & greets in the park, these are unique encounters for hotel guests and have shorter lineups.

- There is now a Starbucks near the Hotel Cheyenne. This Starbucks outlet will be more convenient (read: have less queues) than the Disney Village Starbucks if you need your morning dose and are staying at the Hotel Cheyenne or Hotel Santa Fe.

- As of right now, there is no night parade at Disneyland Paris. Its final procession was called Fantillusion.

- Numerous amiable ghosts and "pumpkin people" overrun Main Street and

Frontierland as part of Disney's Halloween Festival.

- In addition to these entertaining photo opportunities, there is a Halloween parade and a stage production that focuses on villains.

- My favorite backstory for any place, anywhere, is the one for Thunder Mesa. You'll appreciate Frontierland's details more if you read it.

- You'll love Disneyland Paris more if you have a better appreciation for the park's details and background.

- The best book for this purpose is Disneyland Paris: Sketch to Reality. Unfortunately, the price of that out-of-print book is prohibitive.

- The excellent substitute is Disneyland Paris: A to Z. It's also a nice movie to watch this guided tour with Imagineer Tony Baxter.

- Policies change, but so do the ways in which Cast Members interpret them.

- If a Cast Member tells you something that doesn't seem right, be nice, but think about checking with another Cast Member to be sure they're telling you the truth.

- Winter/spring sees the Frozen Celebration at Disneyland Paris and summer sees the Lion King Jungle Festival.

Chapter 8

DISNEYLAND PARks

The Sleeping Beauty Castle, a magnificent centerpiece of the Disneyland Park and one of its five enchanting areas, is well-known around the globe as the beginning of every Disney animated film.

When they first see this magnificent castle, the imposing landmark that welcomes you to the world of dreams, little faces will light up!

Attractions
Pirates of the Caribbean: Board the ship with the infamous movie characters as you go with

Captain Jack Sparrow in search of his buried treasure.

Hold on tight as you travel around a scary mountain in a rattling minecart down a track covered with dynamite on Big Thunder Mountain, a roller coaster thrill experience!

You'll need the fortitude and daring of Indiana Jones to embark on this exhilarating roller coaster ride around jungle ruins called Indiana JonesTM and the Temple of Peril.

Launch yourself into the Star Wars universe at Star Wars Hyperspace Mountain for an exciting takeover of a traditional space attraction.

Enter the magnificent Phantom Manor, a haunted house full of eerie surprises and spooky mysticism.

Prepare to be astounded by Mickey's Philharmagic, a stunning 4D musical experience that transports you to the world of Mickey Mouse and the gang, one of Disney's original characters.

In this interstellar laser-shooting gallery, Buzz Lightyear can launch into space and beat Zurg.

Fly through the air in a magical ship over starry London on your way to Never Land, where mermaids, Indians, and pirates await, in Peter Pan's Flight.

Shows Disney Illuminations - in honor of Disneyland Paris' 30th anniversary, this breathtaking nighttime extravaganza will round off your action-packed day with an amazing fireworks display. Additionally, the sky will be illuminated by a kaleidoscope of sparkles and the epic scores to some of Disney's most beloved productions, including Frozen, The Lion King, Star Wars, and Pirates of the Caribbean!

The Lion King: Rhythms of the Pride Land is an all-singing, all-dancing, exclusive musical production that lets you recreate the most memorable scenes from one of the most beloved films of all time. (Anyone with an entry ticket is welcome, but there may not be enough room.)

The magic will fill the air when the internationally renowned Disney Stars on Parade travels through Disneyland Park. Enjoy the charming music while seeing the characters on their vibrant floats.

Park at Walt Disney Studios
You will plunge right into the thick of the action here! In this theme park, where Disney's cartoons are the main focus, you take center stage and feel as though you're living the movies rather than just viewing them.

ATTRACTIONS

Waltz down Hollywood Boulevard and see Disney Studio 1, a breathtaking recreation of the Tinseltown studios where all the famous characters are brought to life.

Get caught up in the swirling ride that is this fantastic replica of the exciting sequence from Finding NemoTM on Crush's Coaster.

The Malevolent Machine, The Shaft Creatures, and The 5th Dimension are three of the Twilight Zone's three hair-raising horrors that will make you scream yourself stupid.

Children will enjoy the chance to exercise their imagination and learn how to sketch their favorite characters at the Animation Academy.

Worlds of Pixar Cars
In this vibrant world filled with attractions and shows that include your favorite characters from Toy Story, Finding Nemo, Cars, The Incredibles, and more, Pixar's beautiful animations come to life.

Cars Road Trip: Unwind on this journey along the fabled CarsTM highway while taking in the gorgeous surroundings.

Shrink down to Remy's size in Ratatouille: The Adventure and duck, dive, dodge, and scurry to safety on an exciting chase across a mammoth kitchen.

Join the Toy Story recruits in this breath-taking parachute drop behind enemy lines while holding on to your hats!

Selfie Spots in Toon Plaza are designated locations where you may take pictures of your favourite characters dressed to the nines.

And a whole lot more!..

All heroes are needed! Prepare yourself for the grand launch of a brand-new area at Disneyland Paris, packed with exhilarating rides, immersive activities, and stunning, futuristic settings.

Regardless of which of the two parks you choose to enjoy, you will undoubtedly have the most amazing day of fun! The only challenging element is choosing which…

Taking a family vacation? Are timeless rides and iconic characters more your style? Next, we advise choosing Disneyland Park.

More adults and teenagers in your group? Do you enjoy learning about the behind-the-scenes action, cutting-edge animation scenes, and blockbuster characters? Older thrill-seekers should visit Walt Disney Studios Park.

What Will Be Added To Disneyland Paris In 2024 And 2025?

This year, Disneyland Paris is undergoing many changes in preparation for the 2024 Summer Olympics. This update includes what's new, forthcoming, and upcoming in terms of new attractions, shows, special events, and even hotels until 2025 if you're considering visiting Disney's two theme parks in France!

Before I begin, it is important to note that this piece will solely discuss new and altering aspects of Walt Disney Studios Park and Disneyland Paris.

The purpose of this article isn't really to provide an answer to the query of when is the best time to visit Disneyland Paris. Many of you who are reading this are either Europeans who consider DLP to be your "home" resort or are considering including Disneyland Paris in a trip they are already planning to France. Go now in each of those scenarios.

Waiting is advised if this will be a once-in-a-lifetime vacation for long-time Disney fans living outside of Europe who have Disneyland Paris on their bucket list and a very flexible time window for going. By 2025, Walt Disney Studios Park will have improved. Even yet, the advise is dubious because a large portion of what is included in the Walt Disney Studios Park renovation will be exact replicas of what is already (or soon will be) present at Walt Disney World and Disneyland.

The multi-year, $2.5 billion expansion of Disneyland Paris is the next major event, and it will be finished in part by 2023. This is effectively a redesign of the Walt Disney Studios Park, with modifications being introduced over the coming years in stages. The final product was supposed to make its debut in time for the Paris Summer Olympics in 2024...However, it's currently improbable that the project's "meat" would open until 2025.

Looking ahead to the months ahead, the Disneyland Paris 30th Anniversary has just finished a multi-year run. This party was a big success and ought to serve as the model for future get-togethers in theme parks all across the world, not just Disneyland Paris.

Disneyland Paris will end 2023 with celebrations of Halloween and Christmas. After then, it's likely that Disneyland Paris will shift gears once more, working to finish simpler entertainment and placemaking initiatives that will aid in capacity and marketing for the Paris Summer 2024 Olympic Games. (As was mentioned above, the most of the significant additions that were slated to occur have been postponed until 2025.)

What else is new and coming to Disneyland Paris in 2024 or 2025 now that the immediate future has been addressed?

NEAR & FUTURE ADDITIONS

Avengers Campus (Now Open) - A new Marvel-themed area called Avengers Campus, which differs differently from the counterparts in Hong Kong and California, is located in Walt Disney Studios Park. The Avengers Campus at Walt Disney Studios Park is officially open.

The updated Rock 'n' Roller Coaster, which includes Iron Man and the Avengers, is a feature of this new Marvel Land. The Worldwide Engineering Brigade interactive Spider-Man attraction is the second major appeal in addition to that. Through its attractions, hero encounters, and new restaurants, Avengers Campus aims to engage visitors in action-packed adventures.

The newly opened stage play "Together: A Pixar Musical Adventure" at Walt Disney Studios Park takes you on a journey through the fantastic worlds of Toy Story, Monsters, Inc., Finding Nemo, and many more Pixar films.

The idea is that a youngster imagines leading the orchestra in a school play at the conclusion of the year. On the night before the event, though, something goes awry and he misplaces the priceless sheet music. When he nods off, several personalities come to life and perform medleys to recoup the scores. It is just a montage show with a passably engaging narrative thread acting as the binding agent.

Disneyland Paris will soon host a brand-new nightly performance called Disney Symphony of Colours in 2024! This will resemble Disney D-Light but won't take the place of Disney Dreams as Disneyland Paris' primary nighttime show.

The concept art for Disney Symphony of Colours' "electric parade in the sky" phase, which includes a drone sequence modelled after the famous Main Street Electrical Parade, is shown above. This will combine fountains, lights, and projections to fill the sky with a spectrum of bright colours this winter. Launch day for Disney Symphony of Colours is January 8, 2024.

Ahsoka in Star Tours (2024) - In the spring of 2024, Disneyland Paris will introduce Ahsoka as a character in Star Tours: The Adventures Continue.

Not technically breaking news, but this should be a pleasant little update given that Disneyland Paris is severely lacking in new attractions (and will no longer be receiving Star Wars: Galaxy's Edge). Star Tours is still a great attraction, and these upgrades help keep it current.

Kingdom of Arendelle (Probable 2025 Debut): As part of the Walt Disney Studios Park's multi-year expansion, a new themed area devoted to the classic tale of Frozen will open in the coming years.

Visitors will see the snow-capped mountain of Arendelle in the distance opposite a sizable lake as part of the fully immersive area, and a boat journey will take them to Arendelle, as shown in the new concept art above. Character encounters, a brand-new eatery, and a store will also be present.

This Frozen Land's launch date has not yet been specified, although delays due to several slowdowns over the past few years have resulted in a large delay. Although it seems like The Kingdom of Arendelle is a project that is moving quickly at Disneyland Paris, this is insufficient to reach its initial opening date.

A Lakeside Art Nouveau Restaurant is Scheduled to Open in 2025 - Visitors will travel down a promenade surrounded by rich landscapes, a combination of themed gardens and green walks, to approach the new Kingdom of Arendelle Frozen Land. The ambiance of the

Park will be completely changed by this area, which will act as a transition between the new themed areas that will surround the future lake.

The centrepiece of this expansion area will be a classy lakefront restaurant with 250 seats that offers table service. The restaurant's Art Nouveau architecture will provide stunning lake vistas and unique opportunities for character meet-and-greets.

Reimagining Disney Village (2024 and Beyond) - New restaurants, as well as updated retail and entertainment options, will be added to Disney Village over the next years. With a staged redevelopment of the entire region, this 428,000 square foot facility will also receive an aesthetic makeover. This will give the neighbourhood a fresh new look and introduce exciting new services.

The newly designed Disney Village will honour enduring, amiable settings that are exclusively

Disney. Stylish shops and cutting-edge restaurants will entice visitors during the day. By night, the area will be transformed into a busy wonderland by hundreds of lights. Disney Village will have a tranquil lakeside park and boardwalk, improved pedestrian paths, brand-new facades, unwinding terraces and patios, and lush landscaping after the renovation is finished. With cutting-edge ideas from some of the most intriguing brands in the globe, its different eateries and assortment of stores will increase the dining and retail possibilities for visitors.

Rosalie French Brasserie - The current Café Mickey restaurant will be replaced as part of the transformation plan by a modern French brasserie. Groupe Bertrand has been chosen to take over the space and introduce a brand-new concept that will both elevate the eating experience and increase dining options for visitors looking for French flavours in Disney Village. Groupe Bertrand has a network of well-known Parisian brasseries.

Rosalie, a brand-new restaurant with two floors and 500 seats, will have modern decor. It will honour renowned French "Art de Vivre" and classic food in a contemporary yet beautiful setting, with extended terraces overlooking Lake Disney, and is inspired by Parisian brasseries. Along with table service, a counter will provide take-out options inspired by French bakeries, including viennoiseries, pastries, sandwiches, and salads, as well as an array of goods to suit every taste and degree of service.

Imaginative Resorts

Disney Princess-inspired royalty will be celebrated at the historic Disneyland Hotel, which is currently closed for an extensive renovation at Disneyland Paris. The design of the hotel's common areas and the amenities in the rooms will be improved in addition to the redesign of the rooms. A bigger pool area, a bigger spa, and modernised restaurants and lounges will be helpful to visitors. All of which are intended to give the Disneyland Hotel a five-star rating.

The ambitious remodelling programme for all the hotels at Disneyland Paris will continue with this comprehensive renovation, which will include years of work and more than 5,700 rooms. In advance of the Paris Summer Olympics in 2024, Disneyland Paris has made a significant investment in upgrading the guest experience and the resort, as seen by the ambitious renovation plan. For more information, see Opening Date, Concept Art, Room & Restaurant Details of the Reimagined Disneyland Hotel in Paris!

The Art of Marvel at Disney's Hotel New York At Disneyland Paris, this newly redesigned hotel is now open. In a traditional New York setting with a modern Art Deco design, Disney's Hotel New York — The Art of Marvel honours 80 years of Marvel storytelling.

In order to pay homage to the city that is the birthplace of many well-known Marvel characters as well as the artists who developed them, the hotel was modelled after a New York art museum. With one of the greatest publicly viewable collections of Marvel art in the world, Disney's Hotel New York — The Art of Marvel will be the first hotel solely devoted to the celebration of Marvel art when it reopens next summer.

For Disney's Hotel New York — The Art of Marvel, Disneyland Paris worked with more than 50 Marvel Comics and Studios artists to produce 300+ pieces of artwork, including comic book covers, posters, movie poster images, storyboards, original sketches, and more.

As you may be aware, the Hotel New York has been wholly shuttered throughout this rethinking. This reimagining will bring about completely refurbished guest rooms with a contemporary flair, showcasing Marvel artwork in each room and a subtly tribute to the illustrious Iron Man in all Empire State Club rooms. There will be character-themed suites, such as Avengers and Spider-Man.

The first hotel where visitors can have epic encounters with recognisable Marvel super heroes in a unique setting called Super Hero Station is Disney's Hotel New York — The Art of Marvel. There will be exclusive Marvel photo settings, including the Collector's Collection from the Guardians of the Galaxy, Thor's hammer, and more, in addition to the morning meet & greets.

Even if this isn't how we'd like to see the resort reimagined, the Art Deco design is attractive and the artwork seems to have been tastefully included into the plan. Additionally, Hotel New York's former "Big Apple" incarnation was horribly out of date and worn out, and it sorely needed something.

The reinvented Newport Bay Club Hotel, which we recently visited and evaluated, is another relatively recent development.

New and extended seasonal events have also been popular since they served as a bridge while the new expansions were being opened.

RELATIVELY RECENT ADDITIONS

The Disneyland Paris crew created Mickey's Dazzling Christmas Parade in secrecy, and it made its premiere last Christmas. Five enormous floats, including Mickey & Friends, Disney Princesses, Santa Claus & Tinker Bell, and other characters, make up Mickey's Dazzling Christmas Parade.

Each of these floats in Mickey's Dazzling Christmas Parade depicts a charming holiday scene with classic ornaments, and the parade participants will be decked out in dazzling costumes especially created for the event.

Frozen: A Musical Invitation – Located in the Animation Celebration at Walt Disney Studios Park, this brand-new interactive experience whisks visitors away to the Kingdom of Arendelle.

Visitors can connect with their favourite characters on several stages during Frozen: A Musical Invitation. Visitors sing and dance with Anna, Kristoff, and Sven in the first chamber. The second area will transport guests into the ice palace where they will join Elsa in singing the theme song, Let It Go.

Studio D is an additional addition to Walt Disney Studios Park. Mickey, Minnie, and other Disney Junior companions are here to welcome kids and their families to a brand-new interactive show.

For young children, Studio D is a small-scale production similar to a dance party where they can sing and dance with their favourite Disney characters.

Initiative Sparkle, a resort-wide improvement initiative intended to restore the parks to

Disney standards, is the most recent endeavour at Disneyland Paris.

The Walt Disney Company acquired all outstanding shares in Disneyland Paris a few years ago, becoming the sole owner and operator of the park. One of the main driving forces behind the aforementioned $2.5 billion investment is the latter.

Phantom Manor, Big Thunder Mountain Railroad, Star Tours, Pirates of the Caribbean, Space Mountain, 'it's a small world', and other attractions had extensive renovations as a result of Project Sparkle.

Overall, Walt Disney Studios Park and Disneyland Paris have a bright future. There will be a tonne of seasonal events in the near future to keep visitors entertained as they wait for the big items to start appearing between now and 2025. As mentioned above, (parts of) Avengers Campus will make its debut first, and after that, it's anticipated that the Frozen Land

and a version of Star Wars: Galaxy's Edge would come next. We are enthusiastic about the future of Disney's resort complex in France and will be watching it with interest as it develops and grows.

Printed in Great Britain
by Amazon